Jeff Foxworthy's

COMPLETE
REDNECK
DICTIONARY

Jeff Foxworthy's

COMPLETE
REDNECK
DICTIONARY

*All the Words You Thought
You Knew the Meaning Of*

JEFF FOXWORTHY

with FAX BAHR, ADAM SMALL,
GARRY CAMPBELL, AND BRIAN HARTT

Illustrations by LAYRON DeJARNETTE

VILLARD NEW YORK

Published in the United States by Villard Books, an imprint of The Random House Publishing Group, a division of Random House, Inc., New York.

VILLARD and "V" CIRCLED Design are registered trademarks of Random House, Inc.

This work consists of three volumes originally published separately by Villard Books, an imprint of The Random House Publishing Group, a division of Random House, Inc., as *Jeff Foxworthy's Redneck Dictionary: Words You Thought You Knew the Meaning Of* (2005), *Jeff Foxworthy's Redneck Dictionary II: More Words You Thought You Knew the Meaning Of* (2006), and *Redneck Dictionary III: Learning to Talk More Gooder Fastly* (2007).

ISBN 978-0-345-50702-0

Printed in the United States of America on acid-free paper

www.villard.com

2 4 6 8 9 7 5 3 1

First Edition

Book design by Susan Turner

Jeff Foxworthy's

COMPLETE
REDNECK
DICTIONARY

ACNE

abil·i·ties (ə-bil´-ət-ēz), *n. and pron.* a statement of charges for services rendered and subsequent action to be taken by a specified male person. *"I don't care if he's broke, Ma, the house payment's **abilities** got to pay."*

ac·cus·tom (ə-kəs´-təm), *n. and v.* to have verbally abused more than one person with profanity. *"Them kids kept swearin' around Mamaw, so **accustom** out."*

ac·ne (ak´-nē), *v. and n.* concerning a male person's behavior and the result of that behavior. *"Once again we took him to a fancy restaurant, and he didn't know how to **acne** made a fool of himself."*

ac·quire (ə-kwīər´), *n.* a group of singers, especially those who perform during religious ceremonies. *"She sings so pretty, she should join **acquire**."*

ac·quit (ə-kwitˊ), *n. and v.* a personal declaration of resignation from an assigned task. *"You ain't firin' me, 'cuz **acquit**!"*

ac·tiv·ist (aktˊ-əv-ist), *v. and conj.* to behave in a certain manner, particularly one based on another reality. *"She seduced me into signing that petition, and now she **activist** she don't know me!"*

ad·e·quate (aˊ-də-kwit), *n. and v.* to have acted with the intention of terminating one's condition of employment. *"**Adequate** if they hadn't given me a raise."*

ad·min·is·ter (at-miˊ-nə-stər), *adj. and n.* a specific clergyman or agent of a government, as designated by the observer. *"I tell ya, **administer** is a good man."*

afar (ə-färˊ), *n.* an object in the state of combustion. *"There's no sense bein' this cold—let's build **afar**."*

ADEQUATE

AIRLINE

af·ford (ə-fòrd´), *n.* an automobile manufactured by the motor company that produced the Model T. *"If I had the money for a car, I'd want to buy **afford**."*

Af·ghan·i·stan (af-gan´-is-stan), *n. and v.* to declare that a certain living organism of Afghani origin has the name Stanley. *"The Dalmatian's called Jerry, but the **Afghanistan**."*

agent (ā´-jənt), *n. and v.* to negate the importance of the length of a thing's existence. *"She may be eighty, but if I'm drunk enough, **agent** make no difference to me."*

air·line (er´-līn), *adv. and v.* concerning the location and dishonesty of the person being addressed or discussed. *"Don't sit **airline** about it, boy . . . tell the truth!"*

Alas·ka (əl-ask´-ə), *n. and v.* to resolve to make an inquiry. *"If I wanna know where to find a polar bear, **Alaska** guy who lives here."*

Aleve (ə-lēv´), *n. and v.* to intend to vacate. *"Sure Aleve, bud . . . soon as I finish off this six-pack."*

al·i·bi (al´-ə-bī), *n. and v.* the predicted future purchases by a male named Albert, Alfred, or Alvin. *"We always invite Al, 'cause **alibi** drinks for everybody."*

al·lo·sau·rus (a´-lə-sȯr´-əs), *n. and v.* to have been visually perceived by someone named Alice. *"I think my wife **allosaurus** go into that motel room together."*

al·lowed (ə-laúd´), *adj.* distinguished by an intense elevation of volume. *"Did you just hear **allowed** noise?"*

al·lure (ə-lür´), *n.* an object used for enticement, with the intention of capturing prey. *"You want to catch a fish, you gotta use **allure**."*

ALLURE

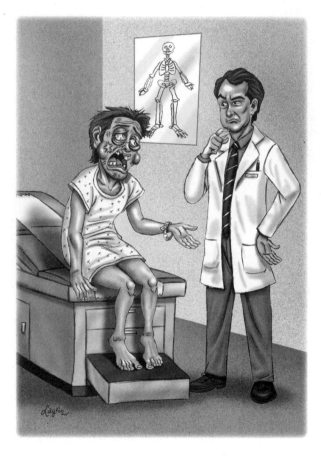

ANARCHIST

an·a·con·da (an-ə-kän´-də), *n. and v.* to have swindled by gaining the confidence of the victim. *"I robbed a bank, stole a car, **anaconda** old lady out of her life savings."*

anal (ān´-òl), *v. and pron.* being inferior to what one expects. *"Enemas **anal** they're cracked up to be."*

an·ar·chist (an-ər-kist´), *conj., n., and v.* additionally, having pressed one's lips to another's as an expression of affection or sensual desire. *"**Anarchist** her ma, **anarchist** her sister, **anarchist** her gramma, **anarchist** her other sister, **anarchist** her other other sister, and then her dad walked in and . . ."*

an·noys (ə-nòiz´), *n.* a loud or irritating sound. *"Well, I wouldn't've peed my pants if I hadn't heard **annoys**!"*

an·nu·al (an´-yü-əl), *n. and v.* regarding the prediction of an action. *"Buy this here Porsche **annual** be dating a lot of ladies."*

an·nu·ity (ə-nü´-ət-ē), *n. and v.* having fore-thought or intuition. *"I couldn't hear him, but* ***annuity*** *was sayin'."*

an·te·lope (ant´-ə-lōp), *n. and v.* the female sibling of one's parent escaping, with the intention of betrothal. *"Sure it's cool to help yer* ***antelope****, but it ain't cool if she's gettin' hitched to you."*

ant·hill (ən-til´), *conj.* up to a point in time. *"I won't set foot in that room* ***anthill*** *he cleans it up!"*

an·ti·pas·to (an´-tē-past-ə), *n. and v.* to discharge from the body, as done by the female sibling of a parent of the speaker. *"After eatin' all that salami last night, my* ***antipasto*** *kidney stone."*

aor·ta (ā-ȯr´-tə), *n. and v.* involving a suggestion for action. *"****Aorta*** *tear that house down and start over."*

AORTA

APPEAL

apart·ment (ə-pärt´-mənt), *adv. and v.* pertaining to one's feelings about a separation. *"Our time together was real good, but the time we were **apartment** a lot more to me."*

ap·par·el (ə-per´-əl), *n. and v.* a prediction concerning the future of two things. *"When it comes to shoes, **apparel** look better than just the one."*

ap·par·ent (ə-per´-ənt), *n.* one who sires or gives birth to offspring. *"It's obvious to me from lookin' at yer belly that yer gonna be **apparent**."*

ap·peal (ə-pēl´), *n.* medicine in a form for oral ingestion. *"I'm sorry, sir, this is not **appeal** you swallow. It's the kind you take rectally."*

ar·chery (ärch´-ər-ē), *n. and conj.* a male person's ultimatum relating to a curved structure, usually one that serves as the roof or overhang of a passageway. *"He went off to St. Louis, sayin' he was dang sure he was goin' to see the **archery** weren't coming back."*

Ar·i·zo·na (er´-əz-ōn-ə), *n., v., and adv.* phrase delimiting the quality of the gaseous atmosphere surrounding the earth. *"I'd move to Denver, but with all the smog that Arizona slightly better than it is here in L.A."*

Ar·kan·sas (ärk´-ən-sȯ), *n. and v.* a flat-bottomed boat in conjunction with an observer's visual perception. *"Noah finished the Arkansas that it was good."*

Ar·ma·ged·don (ärm-ə-ge´-din), *n. and v.* putting oneself in a position for action. *"I tell ya, if it gets any crazier, Armageddon outta here."*

ar·ma·ture (är´-mə-chȯr), *v. and adj.* displaying exceptional wisdom, experience, and/or age. *"I know sometimes I acts like a kid but I really armature."*

ar·rest (ə-rest´), *n.* a state of minimal activity. *"I want the cops to lock me up 'cause, frankly, I could use arrest."*

ARMAGEDDON

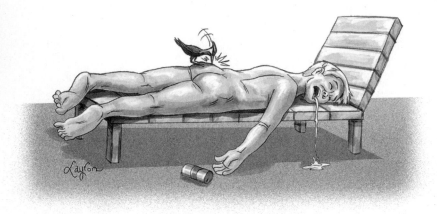

ASPECT

ar·son (ar´-sən), *adj. and n.* pertaining to the male offspring of the speaker. *"I know I swore **arson** didn't set fire to your car, Sheriff, but I guess I misspoke."*

as·cent (ə-sent´), *n. and v.* to have personally dispatched. *"Please don't turn off my phone, dude . . . I swear **ascent** that check three weeks ago!"*

as·i·nine (as´-ə-nīn), *n.* favorable praise of the hind end, to the positive ninth integer. *"Man, I would give her face a two and her **asinine**."*

as·par·a·gus (ə-sper´-ə-gəs), *n.* ambivalence about having to install a replacement for an air-filled rubber wheel. *"I got a flat, so I'm gonna have to put on **asparagus**."*

as·pect (as´-pekt), *n. and v.* having one's backside assaulted by a sharp object. *"He got done skinny-dippin', passed out on that deck chair, and had his **aspect** by a woodpecker."*

ASUNDER

as·sas·sin (ə-sa´-sən), *v.* disrespecting verbally. *"Don't just stand there **assassin** me, boy—go clean your room!"*

asth·ma (az´-mə), *v.* to make an inquiry to a person of familiar acquaintance. *"I don't know if I can go or not. Lemme **asthma** wife."*

asun·der (əs-ən´-dər), *n. and prep.* a gluteal mass situated below or beneath. *"You'll need a tarp-sized blanket to get all of her **asunder** it."*

at·mo·sphere (ət´-məs-fir), *pron. and v.* a conjecture about the feelings of anxiety of a certain being. *"The way that ol' Red tucks his tail, now, that's a dog **atmosphere** his owner."*

at·om (at´-əm), *prep. and n.* in the direction of something or someone. *"Two deer jumped outta the woods and we just started shootin' **atom**."*

ATMOSPHERE

at·tacks (ə-taks´), *n.* a percentage of one's assets taken annually by a governing body. *"If you let 'em, I swear the government would put **attacks** on the air."*

at·tract (ə-trakt´), *v.* to have followed. *"I must **attract** that deer for six miles before I gave up."*

at·trac·tor (ə-trak´-tər), *n.* a motor-propelled machine used mainly in agriculture. *"My uncle cuts his grass with **attractor**."*

Au·di (au´-de), *n.* a protrusion; usually used to describe the knotted flesh on the stomach of a human left after the severing of the umbilical cord. *"Most people have an 'innie,' but Roy's belly button is definitely an **Audi**."*

au·ra (or´-ə), *conj. and adj.* a phrase indicating a choice between one thing and another. *"You gettin' a Quarter Pounder **aura** Big Mac?"*

au·to·mate (ȯ´-tə-māt), *v.* a suggestion for procreation. *"I know we just met tonight, baby, but I think we **automate**."*

av·e·nue (av´-ə-nü), *n. and v.* to declare possession of something recently acquired. *"**Avenue** address, but I don't remember it."*

aw·ful (ȯ-fəl´), *adv. and adj.* satiated gastronomically. *"No dessert for me, thanks, I'm **awful**."*

Bb

ban·dit (band´-ət), *v. and n.* censured or forbidden, by decree. *"We can't dance no more, 'cause after the preacher saw* Footloose, *he **bandit**."*

ban·ner (ban´-ər), *v. and n.* to prohibit a female person from a specific location. *"Cody's grandma cusses so much, they're gonna **banner** from the Little League park."*

AUTOMATE

BARRIER

bar·gain (bär´-gən), *n. and adv.* pertaining to a return to a tavern. *"I'm still thirsty, so whaddya say we go hit that bargain."*

bar·i·um (ber´-ē-əm), *v. and n.* to deposit a male person or animal underground and cover him with earth. *"My dog died yesterday, so we're gonna barium today."*

bar·rel (ber´-əl), *n. and v.* a large, thick-furred, omnivorous mammal of the family Ursidae and its predicted actions. *"A wolverine'll mess you up, but a barrel kill you."*

bar·ri·er (ber´-e-ɔr), *v. and n.* to conceal or cover a female, usually under earth or debris. *"She died while on vacation, so I think they decided to barrier on the beach."*

bas·tards (bas´-tərds), *n.* the fecal excretions of any animal of the Centrarchidae, Serranidae, or Percichthyidae families. *"I'll bet you'll catch a bunch where all them black specks is floatin', 'cause them black specks is bastards."*

bat·tery (ba´-tər-ē), *n. and pron.* a baseball player who regularly attempts an offensive maneuver wherein he uses a club to strike a ball thrown in his direction. *"Stan ain't half the **battery** used to be."*

bay·ou (bī´-ü), *v. and n.* to purchase for another. *"I just walked right up to her and said, 'Hey darlin', lemme **bayou** a drink.'* "

beer (bir´), *v.* to express one's desire to remain at a specific location, usually during intoxication. *"I'll **beer** till ten, then I gotta get home."*

bee·tle (bē´-təl), *v. and conj.* to exist for an unspecified amount of time. *"How long do you think it's gonna **beetle** they figure out we're gone?"*

be·hav·ior (bi-hāv´-yər), *v. and adj.* a phrase connecting the manner in which a person conducts him- or herself to someone or something possessed by or related to that person. *"If you don't **behavior** daddy's gonna spank you!"*

BATTERY

BELIEVE

Bei·rut (bā´-rüt), *adj. and n.* a path that crosses or follows the contours of a broad inlet of water that curves into a landmass. *"I guess old Doug decided to take the **Beirut**."*

be·lieve (bē-lēv´), *n. and v.* a demand for the *Bombus ruderatus* to vacate the immediate vicinity. *"Oh no! I'm allergic! **Believe** me alone!"*

be·moan (bē-mōn´), *v. and adj.* to declare possession by oneself. *"I don't like takin' orders. That's why I gotta **bemoan** boss."*

be·nign (bē-nīn´), *v. and adj.* to reach a level of one increment more than eight. *"The scar from your tumor removal is going to **benign** inches long."*

bet·ter·ment (be´-tər-mənt), *v. aux. and v.* demanding a certain or particular intention. *"I'm not sure I heard you right. You **betterment** that you were gonna marry my little girl."*

big·a·my (big´-ə-mē), *adj. and n.* a boastful proclamation of one's actions as generous. *"It was pretty*
bigamy *to pick up the dinner check for all of my ex-wives."*

big·ots (big´-əts), *adj.* used to describe a large object in motion or action. *"Man, Al's belly is so **bigots***
draggin' on the floor."

bi·son (bī´-sən), *interj. and n.* used to express
farewell to a male offspring. *"The day I went off to*
welding school, Mama stood on the porch with tears in
*her eyes and said, '**Bison**.' "*

bit·ter (bit´-ər), *v. and n.* involving the closing of
jaws, as done on a female. *"She kept teasin' that dog till*
*he finally **bitter**."*

bob·ble (bäb´-əl), *n. and v.* the confident prediction
for future action, to be effected by a person named
Robert. *"Don't worry, Marge. **Bobble** get us out of here."*

BOBBLE

BOMBARDIER

bob·sled (bäbs´-led), *n. and v.* the act of guidance by a person named Robert. *"I ain't no expert, but I think bobsled us down the wrong path."*

boil (böi´-əl), *interj. and v.* a term preceding a prediction. *"Boil they be surprised when they find out I ain't dead."*

bom·bar·dier (bamb´-ə-dir), *v. and n.* to attack an *Odocoileus virginianus* with an explosive device. *"When I'm huntin' I usually use my rifle, but sometimes I just take out dynamite and bombardier."*

bor·der (bör´d-ər), *v. and n.* to have made a female feel uninterested and fatigued, as through tedious action or talk. *"She said she left him because he border to death."*

bor·row (bär´-ō), *n. and v.* a phrase concerning the future state of a tavern. *"Hurry up or the borrow be closed!"*

bot·a·ny (bät´-ən-ē), *v. and conj.* used to describe the reaction of a male person to a purchase, usually by his spouse. *"When she got back from the mall, she showed him what she botany killed himself."*

bot·tle (bät´-əl), *n. and v.* the corporeal form of a being and its future state. *"If you keep eatin' and drinkin' like that, your bottle go bad."*

boy·sen·berry (böiz-ən-ber´-ē), *n., conj., and v.* a phrase connecting a group of males to the act of interring a being or thing underground. *"Get the boysenberry this guy before the cops show up."*

brid·al (brīd´-əl), *n. and v.* a betrothed female and her future state. *"If the preacher don't move it along, the bridal have her baby right there on the altar."*

bro·ker (brōk´-ər), *v. and adj.* to have violently injured any thing or things belonging to a female. *"My mom fell off a ladder and broker arm."*

BOTTLE

BULLETIN

bud·get (bəj´-ət), *v. and n.* to transfer an object from one location to another. *"Papaw was workin' on my car and it fell on his foot. I tried to pull it off, but I couldn't budget!"*

bu·lim·ia (bəh-lē´-mē-ə) *v. and n.* a demand that one accept the speaker's truthfulness. *"Bulimia don't want to eat that again."*

bul·le·tin (bü´-lət-in), *n. and prep.* a metal projectile intended for use in a firearm and its position with relation to the interior of an object. *"If you want to save us, you're gonna have to put a bulletin that gun."*

bur·den (bərd´-in), *n. and prep.* indicating the specific location of a flying creature. *"A burden the hand is worth two in the bush."*

butch·er (bü´-chər), *v. and adj.* to place or lay an object or objects belonging to another. *"If you don't want a fist in your face, you better butcher cards on the table."*

but·ter (bət´-ər), *conj. and adj.* with the exception of an action by or quality of a female. *"She may be nice on the eyes, **butter** cookin'll kill ya."*

but·ter·fly (bət-ər-flī´), *conj. and n.* an exception concerning the opening in pants worn by a female. *"I didn't mean to embarrass her, **butterfly** was open!"*

but·ton fly (bət´-in-flī), *n. and v.* to elevate one's posterior above the ground. *"The mother bird just told her baby to get off its **button fly**."*

cab·i·net (kab´-ən-it), *n.* used in reference to an event taking place within a vehicle employed for ferrying passengers. *"When we were in New York, we got in a **cabinet** stunk!"*

ca·chet (ka-shā´), *n. and pron.* currency, in relation to a group of people. *"He spent every cent of the **cachet** gave him before he got kicked out of that casino."*

BUTTER

CAJOLE

ca·dav·er (kəd-av´-ər), *v. and adj.* pertaining to the possibility of gaining possession of something belonging to a female. *"The coroner had to get back to the morgue, but she said I cadaver fries."*

Cae·sar (sēz´-ər), *v. and n.* to visually perceive a female. *"He has a seizure every time he Caesar."*

ca·jole (kə-jól´), *v. and n.* a request for action from a group. *"I don't like being the center of attention, so cajole stop staring at me?"*

Ca·jun (kāj´-ən), *n. and conj.* an enclosed space used to confine a being, especially as connected with an action. *"They just threw that bear in a Cajun left him there."*

Cal·cut·ta (kal-kət´-ə), *n. and v.* (*usu. vulgar*) the release of intestinal gas by a person named Calvin. *"Well, far as I can tell, Calcutta fart and then somebody struck a match."*

Can·a·da (kan´-ə-də), *n. and prep.* a metal container with specific contents. *"Do me a big favor, bud, and hand me a Canada bug spray."*

can·cel (kant´-səl), *v.* the inability to exchange property for money. *"If you cancel that hunk of crap, I'll take it off your hands."*

can·cer (kan´-sər), *v. and n.* to formally acknowledge one's abilities. *"He asked if I could be there by eight o'clock and I said, 'Yes, I cancer.' "*

can·dy (kand´-ē), *v. and n.* negative verb for a male unable to act. *"Why candy just ask you one simple question?"*

can·nel·lo·ni (kan-əl-ō´-nē), *n. and v.* the limit to a metal container's capacity. *"That cannelloni hold about two cups of water."*

CANADA

CANTALOUPE

can·ni·bal (kan´-ə-bŭl), *v. and n.* interrogative concerning the abilities of an uncastrated male bovine. *"I've always wondered, **cannibal** mate with more than one cow in a day?"*

can·o·py (kan-ə-pē´), *n.* a metal vessel used for the containment of urine. *"The dude never stops for bathroom breaks. That's why there's a **canopy** in his truck."*

can·ta·loupe (kant´-ə-lōp), *v.* the expressed inability to marry in secret. *"My daddy wants a traditional marriage, honey, so I **cantaloupe**."*

can·ter (kan´-tər), *v. and adj.* negative interrogative concerning the abilities of someone connected to a female. *"**Canter** sister watch the baby?"*

can·ti·le·ver (kant´-ə-lēv-ər), *v. and n.* to inquire about the possibilities for ending a relationship. *"The preacher said till death do us part, but **cantilever** if she fools around on me?"*

can·ti·na (kan-tē´-nəh), *v. and n.* interrogative concerning the actions or abilities of a person who uses a nickname for Christine. *"Hey, **cantina** bring us a couple of cold beers?"*

ca·pa·ble (kāp´-ə-bŭl), *n., adj., and n.* a garment that ties at the neck and hangs across the back and its association with an uncastrated male bovine. *"Soon as he sees a red **capable** will attack."*

cap·i·tal (kap´-ət-il), *n. and v.* regarding an action concerning the future of any covering used to close off a receptacle. *"Careful with that bottle—if you don't put on that **capital** spill."*

car·cass (kär´-kəs), *n. and conj.* the reason for an action or event related to a motor vehicle. *"My daddy won't let me drive his **carcass** I've hit too many deer."*

car·di·gan (kärd-ə-gin), *n. and adv.* repeated action upon or using a small, rectangular piece of cardboard adorned with rank and suit. *"Something's fishy with this deck, 'cause you just played the same **cardigan**."*

CARDIGAN

CARGO

car·go (kär´-gō), *n. and v.* an automobile moving on a certain course, usually forward. *"Can't you make this cargo any faster?"*

cash·ew (ka´-shü), *v. and n.* to exchange chips for hard currency. *"I wanted to keep gambling, but the manager said, 'I think we'd better cashew in.' "*

cash·ier (kash´-ir), *n.* any medium for fiscal exchange, in a specific place. *"I tried to pay by check, but the lady behind the register told me they only take cashier."*

ca·si·no (kəs-ē´-nō), *conj. and v.* a phrase concerning a gentleman with particular knowledge. *"When I go to Vegas, I go with my buddy Roy, casino more about gamblin' than I do."*

cas·trate (kast´-rāt), *n.* a hardened plaster mold used for immobilizing a broken limb so that the bone will not heal crookedly. *"They're gonna have to rebreak my arm 'cause they said the doctor didn't get the castrate the first time."*

CAT scan (kats´-kan), *n. and v.* pertaining to the abilities of members of the feline family. *"No way my dogs are getting on this here couch, but my CAT scan."*

cat·e·go·ry (kat´-ə-gȯr-ē), *n. and adj.* a domesticated feline bleeding profusely from excessive trauma. *"That guy hit Fluffy goin' fifty miles an hour and left that category mess."*

cat·tle (kat´-əl), *n. and v.* a feline creature and its future actions. *"Be careful, that old cattle scratch your eyes out if you get anywhere near her."*

cau·li·flow·er (kȯl´-ə-flau-ər), *v. and n.* to verbally describe the reproductive organs of an angiospermous plant. *"You can't cauliflower anything but beautiful."*

cau·ter·ize (kȯt´-ər-īz), *v. and n.* to visually engage a female person's ocular organs. *"It was love at first sight the second I cauterize."*

CAT SCAN

cel·lar (sel´-ər), *v. and adj.* to trade a thing in a female's possession for currency. *"My sister is so broke she had to **cellar** entire collection of fine wines."*

cel·lu·lite (sel´-yü-līt), *v. and adj.* to make a mercantile exchange wherein a food or beverage product of reduced caloric content is traded for currency. *"We're outta regular Bud, but I could **cellulite** beer."*

cen·sure (sent´-shər), *conj. and v.* pertaining to an ongoing condition of the person addressed. *"I'll have another drink, **censure** payin'."*

cen·ter (sent´-ər), *v. and n.* to urge, instruct, or propel a female into action. *"Soon as she started in with her naggin' I **center** packing."*

cen·ti·me·ter (sent´-ə-mē-tər) *v. and n.* to be ordered or instructed to await the arrival of a female person. *"My gramma's coming in on the train, and I been **centimeter**."*

CERTIFY

cer·ti·fy (sər´-təf-ī), *n. and conj.* a phrase applying a condition or assumption to the use of a formal term for a male person. *"I wouldn't've called her **certify** had known it was a woman."*

chap·ter (chapt´-ər), *v. and adj.* to have received epidermal roughening. *"That wind **chapter** lips up pretty good."*

char·i·ty (char´-ə-tē), *n. and pron.* a restrictive clause relating to a male person's actions concerning a piece of furniture providing an individual seat. *"That fat boy breaks every **charity** sits in."*

chauf·feur (shō´-fər), *n. and prep.* a reference to a performance. *"There's nekkid girls inside, boys, and I can get you into the **chauffeur** just two dollars!"*

chick·en (chik´-in), *n. and conj.* a connection between a female person and something else. *"I went to the movies with that **chicken** Maynard . . . next thing I know, we was makin' out."*

CHAPTER

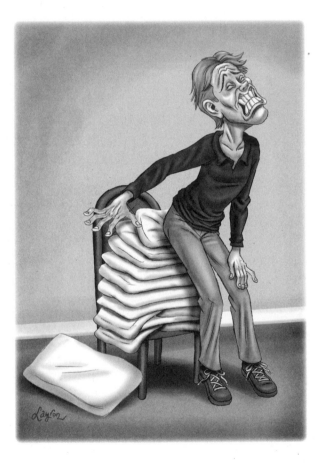

CITY

cin·em·a (sin´-əm-ə), *v. and n.* to cause a thing to be delivered to a male. *"I was so mad at the producer of that movie, I **cinema** letter givin' him a piece of my mind."*

cir·cus (sər´-kəs), *n. and conj.* a formally addressed justification of actions, as spoken to male person. *"I can't refund your money **circus** I don't work here."*

city (sit´-ē), *v. and n.* the act of reclining onto the buttocks, as connected with a male's subsequent response or action. *"On account of his hemorrhoids, every time he tries to **city** screams."*

clar·i·fy (kler´-əf-ī), *adj. and conj.* the dependence of the lucidity of a thing or concept on another condition or action. *"I'm not **clarify** should stay or go."*

clas·si·fied (klas´-əf-īd), *n. and conj.* pertaining to regret over a course at school. *"I'd have gone to **classified** been smarter."*

cli·mate (klīm´-ət), *v. and n.* to ascend a thing. *"Soon as I set my eyes on a mountain, I'm not satisfied till I climate."*

clos·er (klōz´-ər), *v. and adj.* to discontinue or shut something of a female's. *"Please tell her to closer mouth when she eats."*

cof·fee (köf´-ē), *v. and n.* to explosively expel air from the lungs, as performed by a male. *"My granddad's got a cold, and every time he tries to coffee wets his pants."*

colt (kōlt´), *adj.* having an unpleasantly low temperature. *"I'll say it's colt out here, man. . . . When I got back to the barn, my dang horse was frozen solid!"*

col·umn (käl´-əm), *v. and n.* an imperative regarding electronic communication with a specific male. *"Daddy likes you best, dude, so you column."*

COLUMN

co·ma (kōm´-ə), *v.* to groom hair using a multi-toothed tool. *"When you're a barber you have to **coma** lot of ugly heads."*

com·fort (kəm´-fərt), *v. and adv.* to move toward, with the aim of procurement. *"That fellah that left his dog here . . . I hope he'll **comfort** soon."*

com·i·cal (kä´-mik-əl), *n. and v.* a person whose profession is causing amusement and his or her future actions. *"That **comical** make you laugh your head off."*

con·ceal (kən-sēl´), *v.* to be able to cover tightly. *"If you **conceal** up that window, a lot less bugs'll get in."*

con·ceit (kən-sēt´), *v.* to be able to accommodate resting places for buttocks. *"Our high school football stadium **conceit** fifty thousand."*

CONDOM

con·dom (känd´-əm), *v. and n.* having purpose-fully swindled a gullible male for personal gain. *"She condom into thinkin' she was on the pill."*

con·sid·er (kən-sid´-ər), *v. and n.* to be capable of placing a female in the position of resting on her but-tocks. *"Sure Ma's senile, but I consider down in the park for hours while I go to the casino."*

con·spire (kən-spīr´), *v. aux. and v.* to perceive a fe-male through the ocular organs. *"With them stupid hats she wears, I conspire comin' a couple of blocks away."*

con·stab·u·lary (kän-stab´-ū-lar-ē), *n. and v.* the capability of a convicted criminal to use a sharpened object to wound the flesh of a person named Lawrence. *"You can't work at the prison if you keep let-ting some constabulary."*

con·trol (kən-trōl´), *v.* to be able, while moving slowly, to display a lure for the purpose of capture. *"You control in this lake for a week, and you still ain't gonna catch a fish."*

CONSPIRE

COUNTY

con·vey·or (kən-vaʹ-ər), *v. and adj.* to transmit a nonpresent female's communications. *"My wife couldn't be here, but she wanted me to conveyor sympathies."*

cop·per (käpʹ-ər), *n. and conj.* a choice between a law enforcement officer and someone else. *"Any sixth grader with a full beard is either a copper a narc."*

copy (käpʹ-ē), *n. and pron.* regarding an action by a male person concerning a law enforcement officer. *"I hope we don't run into the copy shot at."*

coun·ter·feit (kaůntʹ-ər-fit), *n. and v.* a flat surface used for storage, the transaction of business, or dining, and its dimensions with respect to those of a specific place. *"We shoulda measured the kitchen first, 'cuz no amount of money'll make this counterfeit in there."*

coun·ty (kaůntʹ-ē), *v. and n.* to combine integers, as done by a male person. *"To county has to take off his shoes, if you want him to get past ten."*

cou·ple (kəp´-əl), *n. and v.* an eight-ounce container for measuring liquids and its future state. *"If you wanna party with pure grain, one **couple** do the trick."*

cous·in (kəz´-ən), *conj.* for a reason, specifically relating to a particular place. *"You can't sleep with your relatives, **cousin** the big city that's a crime."*

cra·ter (krā´-tər), *n.* the Supreme Being, responsible for bringing forth all things known and unknown. *"Come Judgment Day, all you sinners are gonna have to answer to the **crater**!"*

crotch·ety (krä´-chət-ē), *n. and pron.* a phrase connecting a male to a place where two things join, as in where the legs meet on the human body. *"I wouldn't be so cranky if it wasn't my **crotchety** hit with a bat."*

Cu·ba (kyü´-bə), *n. and prep.* a three-dimensional square-sided object with relation to the substance that composes it. *"Want me to put a **Cuba** ice in your drink?"*

CROTCHETY

CUTTER

cus·tom (kəst´-əm), *v. and n.* to have voiced vulgar language at a person or persons. *"When them Jehovah's Witnesses came to our house, Granddaddy done custom out."*

cut·ter (kət´-ər), *v. and adj.* to use a sharp instrument to separate one thing from another, as performed by a female. *"If Sheila don't cutter toenails soon, I'm filin' for a divorce."*

Dd

dairy (der´-ē), *v. and n.* the audacity or bravery of a male. *"With that cow Ted's married to, how dairy say something about my wife."*

Da·ko·ta (də-kō´-tə), *n. and v.* a prediction concerning an outer garment worn on the torso. *"It's ten below, man. Dakota keep you warm."*

Da·mas·cus (dəm´-ask-əs), *n. and v.* involving a question posed by more than one person to more than one person. *"**Damascus** where we was the night Toby's Bar burned down, but we didn't say nothin'."*

da·ta (dāt´-ə), *v. and adj.* to undertake an event of social interaction, usually with the purpose of romance. *"I'd never **data** rich girl."*

de·bate (də-bāt´), *n.* anything used to entice prey. *"I don't wanna argue no more 'bout which worm we're gonna use for **debate**."*

deci·bel (des´-ə-bəl), *n. and v.* a declaration that an observed thing is an uncastrated male bovine. *"You ain't getting' any milk from it 'cuz **decibel**."*

de·cide (di-sīd´), *n.* the position to the right or left of the front or back of an object or being. *"We've concluded that he resembles a pear if you look at him from **decide**."*

DEFEAT

DEFINITE

de·feat (di-fēt´), *n.* the lower extremities, upon which a creature ambulates. *"That's gonna be one big dog, judgin' by the size of defeat."*

de·fend·er (di-fen´-dər), *n.* a metal guard positioned over the wheel of a motor vehicle. *"The grille's okay, but defender is torn up real bad."*

de·fense (di-fents´), *n.* a barrier bisecting a piece of land. *"I told him to drive through da gate and the damn dummy drove through defense."*

de·fined (di-fīnd´), *n.* an unexpected discovery. *"That old dictionary you got at the yard sale is defined of the century."*

def·i·nite (def´-ən-it), *adj. and n.* of or pertaining to a person who is hearing impaired. *"My grandma's real definite affects the odds on her life expectancy."*

de·lights (di-līts´), *n.* electrical devices used for illumination. *"Hey, stupid, turn out **delights**."*

de·liv·er (di-li´-vər), *n.* a large, glandular organ in the body that assists in the metabolic process. *"Considering how much our mailman drinks, I don't know how **deliver** on him holds up."*

de·mand·ed (dih-man´-did), *n. and v.* a male person's past actions. *"It ain't right they fired him, 'cuz **demanded** everything they told him to."*

de·men·tia (dim-ent´-shə), *n. and v.* interrogative concerning one's reaction to, or connection with, more than one person. *"You lookin' at **dementia**?"*

de·mo·graph·ic (dem-ə-gra´-fik), *n. and adj.* referring to visually explicit material. *"**Demographic** photos in that dirty magazine."*

DEMENTIA

DESCENT

dem·on·strate (dem´-ən-strāt), *n. and adj.* in a linear fashion. *"Your glasses are all crooked, girl . . . put demonstrate."*

den·i·grate (den´-i-grāt), *adv. and adj.* a reference to the ensuing occurrence of something large and/or wondrous. *"First my stomach hurt, and denigrate wind came outta my rear end, and now I feel a whole lot better."*

den·tal (dent´-əl), *n. and v.* to do with the result of a crease or a depression in all types of metal plating. *"Well, the good news is that little dental come out real easy."*

de·scent (di-sent´), *n.* an olfactory emission. *"The dogs lost descent right about here."*

de·sign (di-zīn´), *n.* a poster or board that identifies, advertises, warns, or indicates the purpose of a thing. *"And design said long-haired freaky people need not apply."*

DESIGN

de·spair (dis-per´), *adj. and n.* a particular set of two of something. *"Despair is the best hand I had all night."*

de·tail (di-tāl´), *n.* an appendage extending from the buttocks, usually covered with hair. *"Best way to catch a skunk is just to grab him by detail."*

de·ten·tion (di-ten´-chən), *n.* special notice taken of a person or thing. *"Detention he gives that woman just makes you sick."*

de·void (di-void´), *n.* an absence of matter. *"Devoid that woman left in my heart is as big as a truck."*

di·al (dī´-əl), *v. and n.* a phrase connecting the possible termination of life to the speaker. *"If your fish dial be devastated."*

di·et (dī´-ət), *v. and n.* to change the hue of some-thing. *"You know what you oughta do with your hair, Barb, is diet red."*

di·gest (dī´-jest), *v. and adv.* to expire, especially recently. *"I don't know why Daddy had to digest three days after Mama."*

di·late (dī´-lāt), *v. and adv.* to experience the termi-nation of life well into a specified temporal period. *"I hope I dilate in life."*

di·lem·ma (də-le´-mə), *prep. and n.* a phrase con-necting an action up to a certain point in time with a person named Emma. *"Wait dilemma gets home and finds out you broke her favorite TV."*

di·men·sion (də-men´-shən), *n.* an instance of casually calling attention to something. *"Just dimension of pork and beans makes me gassy."*

DINETTE

di·nette (dīn-ət´), *v. and prep.* to eat supper out, with reference to a specific location. *"I don't want to **dinette** this restaurant ever again."*

di·no·saur (dī´-nə-sȯr) *n., v., and pron.* a person named Dinah having visually perceived something belonging or related to her. *"After she invested in the T. rex museum, **dinosaur** life savings go down the drain."*

di·rec·tion (də-rek´-shən), *n.* the engorgement of the male sex organ. *"Doc, could you give my Hank here a sample of those little blue pills? **Direction** ain't what it used to be."*

dis·abil·i·ty (dis-ə-bi´-lə-tē), *adj. and n.* a certain aptitude or proficiency. *"I was born with **disability** to charm women of the opposite sex."*

dis·arm (dis-ärm´), *adj. and n.* a specified unit, support, or appendage; in particular, the human forelimb. *"I'm goin' to the doctor, 'cuz **disarm** is killing me."*

DIRECTION

DISCO

di·sas·ter (di-sas´-tər), *adv. and v.* a phrase used to persuade someone to inquire something of a female person, by characterizing the inquiry as simple and easy. *"She's bound to break my heart, but I **disaster** out anyway."*

dis·co (dis´-kō), *n. and v.* referring to the intended or proper location of a specific thing; usually used with an inquiry. *Query in operating room: "I put everything else back . . . but now where's **disco**?"*

dis·count (dis-kaünt´), *adv. and v.* to instruct another to merely list numbers consecutively. *"You **discount** to a hundred, and we'll hide."*

dis·cov·er (dis-kə´-vər), *adj. and n.* a particular object on or over something or used to protect it. *"I couldn't find baby Boo for the life of me, till I lifted **discover**."*

dis·cussed (dis-kəst´), *adv. and v.* to have recently used profanity. *"I'm probably gonna get kicked out of school 'cuz my mama discussed out the principal again."*

dis·ease (diz-ēz´), *v. and adj.* interrogative concerning more than one thing. *"I been sick for nine years, Doc. Disease pills work or not?"*

dis·fig·ured (dis-fi´-gyərd), *adv. and v.* to have ascertained. *"I disfigured you would go with me instead of him."*

dis·guise (dis-gīz´), *adj. and n.* a specified male person and his current actions or state. *"I don't think disguise wearing a mask."*

dis·gust·ed (di-skəst´-id), *v. and n.* to have verbally considered or examined a specific subject. *"Billy, your mother and I have disgusted, and we both think you're on steroids."*

DISGUISE

dish·wash·er (dish´-wä-shər), *adv. and v.* a phrase indicating the speaker's desire for a specific female person to merely perform routine ablutions. *"I know the cook doesn't clean her pots, but I wish she'd **dishwasher** hands."*

dis·lo·cat·ed (dis-lō´-kā-təd), *pron. and v.* a thing situated in a specific physical place. *"We need to find the doctor's office **dislocated** on the second floor."*

dis·may (dis-mā´), *n. and v.* something raised as a possibility. *"**Dismay** come as a surprise, ma'am, but you're not pregnant."*

dis·mem·ber (dis-mem´-bər), *adv. and v.* to recall; often used as a plea or an imperative. *"We could butcher that hog if I could **dismember** where I put my cleaver."*

dis·play (dis-plā´), *adv. and v.* to simply participate in a recreational activity. *"Quit whining and **display** the game!"*

DISROBE

dis·robe (dis-rōb´), *adj. and n.* a particular full-length long-sleeved garment, usually worn over pajamas. *"How come you always make me take disrobe off in the dark, sweetie?"*

dis·solve (dis-sälv´), *adv. and v.* to achieve a quick resolution to or completion of a problem. *"You got enough clues, dissolve the dang puzzle!"*

dis·taste (dis-tāst´), *n. and v.* regarding the distinctive flavor of a specific thing. *"Is it just me, or does distaste funny?"*

dis·tress (dis-tres´), *n.* a skirted garment, especially of a full-figured person. *"Does distress make my butt look fat?"*

dis·trict (dis´-trikt), *adv. and adj.* severe in terms of discipline. *"I never woulda joined up if I'd known the army was gonna be district."*

DISSOLVE

DITTY

dit·ty (dit´-ē), *v. and n.* interrogative concerning the past actions of a male person. *"Let me guess: your husband never learned how to swim, **ditty**?"*

di·verse (də-vərs´), *n.* a lyrical, nonrepeating stanza within a song. *"I've got the chorus, but **diverse** is still givin' me trouble."*

doc·tor (däkt´-ər), *v. and adj.* to have applied to a female employee a punitive measure in which a percentage of her wages are garnisheed. *"After my wife wrecked that forklift, they **doctor** pay for the next six months."*

doc·tor·ate (däk´-tər-ət), *v. and n.* to change or modify something. *"We can make your medical résumé look better if we **doctorate** up a little bit."*

doc·u·ment (däk´-yə-mənt), *n. and v.* an intended medical professional. *"First you said Dr. Reynolds did it, and now you're saying that ain't the **document**."*

DOMAIN

dog·ma (dȯg´-mə), *v. and adj.* to personally insult something belonging to one. *"I had to hit him, sir—I ain't just gonna sit there and let a man **dogma** truck."*

dog·wood (dȯg´-wŭd), *n. and v.* the past or conditional actions of a canine. *"I'm in this tree 'cuz otherwise that **dogwood** bite me."*

dol·lar (däl´-ər), *n. and conj.* an alternative between a toy figure in human form and something else. *"Is that cashier a living **dollar** what?"*

do·main (dō-mān´), *v.* to lack importance. *"Don't let it bug you, man. It **domain** a thing."*

doo·dle (düd´-əl), *n. and v.* a male person and his predicted actions. *"Don't even look at him, 'cuz that **doodle** kill you."*

DOODLE

dou·bloon (də-bloon´), *n.* any single object having a hue in the color spectrum between green and vi-
olet. *"You can wear the brown hat or the green hat, but
don't touch **doubloon**."*

doz·en (dəz´-ən), *v. and adv.* the negative or opposite of an expected action or reaction. *"If that **dozen**
make you laugh, then you don't know what's funny."*

drag·on (dra´-gɔn), *v.* being brought into, usually
by force. *"Don't be **dragon** me into your argument."*

drain (drān´), *n.* precipitation. *"**Drain** in Spain falls
mainly on the plain."*

drib·ble (drib´-əl), *n. and v.* a cut of meat including a curved bone protruding from the spine and its
predicted state. *"If you smother it in barbecue sauce,
dribble taste much better."*

DWARF

du·ty (dü´-tē), *v. and n.* to act in the same manner as a specified male. *"If the guy got ya, just **duty** did: light a bag of crap on fire and put it on his porch."*

dwarf (dwȯrf´), *n.* a structure built alongside or on a body of water for the purpose of parking watercraft. *"We can fish down at **dwarf**."*

dy·na·mite (dī´-nə-mīt), *v. and n.* concerning expiration and one's subsequent action or reaction. *"I know blowing up this safe is dangerous. I might **dynamite** not."*

ear (ir´), *v.* to receive and cognitively process sound. *"Huh? I couldn't **ear** a single word you said."*

east·ern (ēs´-tərn), *n. and v.* indicating a change in a male. *"He was a cute baby, but **eastern** into a real monster."*

EASTERN

easy·go·ing (ē-zē-gō´-ing), *v. and n.* interrogative regarding the future movements or trajectory of a male. *"Easygoing to relax or not?"*

ego (ē´-gō), *n. and v.* a male moving from one location to another. *"He's a good man, Daddy . . . ego to church every Sunday."*

Egypt (ē´-jipt), *n. and v.* to have been cheated or swindled by a male. *"Aw, man, Egypt me!"*

eighty (ā´-tē), *v. and n.* a male, after mastication. *"Right after the old guy eighty blew chunks in my car."*

Ei·sen·how·er (ī´-zən-haú-ər), *n. and v.* a personal declaration concerning an action or condition lasting for one twenty-fourth of the earth's revolution on its axis. *"Last time Mamie spent the night, Eisenhower late for work."*

el·der (el´-dər), *v. and n.* to embrace or restrain a female. *"After the old lady mugged us, Junior **elder** down till the cops arrived."*

el·e·gance (el´-i-gəns), *adj. and prep.* a group either in opposition or in close physical proximity. *"They're **elegance** her just 'cuz she's different."*

el·e·ment (el´-ə-mənt), *n. and v.* a clause clarifying or summing up a past statement or action of the speaker's. *"Sorry you thought I'd pay you back today— **element** was I'd pay you back someday."*

elite (il-ēt´), *n. and v.* a phrase predicting ingestion by a male. *"Give it to Jake . . . **elite** anything."*

elix·ir (i-liks´-ər), *n. and v.* the act, by a male mammal, of lapping any specific female with his tongue. *"My dog wakes my daughter up every mornin'. He jumps on the bed and **elixir** face."*

ELIXIR

EMIGRATE

em·bark (im-bärk´), *n. and v.* referring to the production of the short, sharp cry characteristic of the male of the species *Canis familiaris*. *"That dog's so well behaved you can't make embark."*

em·bit·ter (im-bi´-tər), *n. and adj.* when a male feels resentful, angry, vengeful, and soured. *"His divorce just left embitter."*

em·i·grate (em-ə-grāt´), *n. and adj.* an egotistical inquiry. *"I nailed us some pretty good seats here, dude. Emigrate or what?"*

emis·sion (ə-mi´-shən), *n.* an assignment, strongly felt ambition, or calling. *"The way she's drivin' that car, she's on emission to fail the smog test."*

emo·tions (i-mō´-shəns), *n. and v.* to indicate something with gestures, as performed by a male. *"Every time he makes a big play, emotions to the crowd to make more noise."*

en·close (in-klōz´), *n.* attired in garments. *"She looks good enclose, but she looks better out of them."*

en·coun·ter (in-kaún´-tər), *v.* to respond to one offer with another. *"Find out what he's askin' for it encounter with a lower offer."*

en·dive (en-dīv´), *conj. and v.* to leap or plunge, especially in a headlong manner. *"Just walk to the edge of the board endive off."*

en·e·ma (en´-ə-mə), *n. and v.* declaring one's state of being or whereabouts. *"Dang it all! My car broke down, enema good ten miles from a gas station."*

en·roll (in-rōl´), *conj. and v.* to move by revolving or turning over repeatedly. *"I told you, Lloyd, if you catch on fire you're supposed to stop, drop, enroll."*

ENROLL

ERODE

eras·es (i-rā´-səz), *n. and v.* competing in a contest involving speed, especially by any person named Dale Jr. *"Dale Jr. is the man. Erases anybody, anywhere."*

erec·tor (i-rekt´-ər), *n. and v.* to have destroyed or rendered useless; as done by a male. *"Tom's wife is mad at him 'cause erector new car."*

er·go (ər´-gō), *n. and v.* a female moving off on a specific course. *"I want to take my girlfriend camping, but I don't think her dad's gonna let ergo."*

erode (i-rōd´), *n. and v.* a male person on a thing that moved him around physically. *"Old man Wilkins is losing it, dude. Erode that dang pig all the way to town."*

es·ca·la·tor (esk´-ə-lā-tər), *v.* to make a planned or scheduled inquiry. *"I got a question, but I'm kinda busy right now, so could I escalator?"*

es·cape (is-kāp´), *n.* a long, hanging garment worn on a man's back. *"I wouldn't have known he was a superhero, but escape gave him away."*

es·crow (es´-krō), *v.* to suggest the instigation of the natural process wherein a seedling advances in size. *"Escrow some tomatoes this summer."*

es·tate (is-stāt´), *adj. and n.* a male person's psychological status or condition. *"I wouldn't trust him in estate of mind."*

eu·pho·ria (yü-fȯr´-ē-ə), *n.* form of address for a group consisting of a number of persons between three and five. *"Hey! Euphoria ain't going nowhere till you clean up that mess!"*

Eu·phra·tes (yü-frāt´-ēz), *n. and adj.* to be in fear of bodily harm from a male. *"What's the matter, Timmy? Euphrates gonna hit ya?"*

ESTATE

EXHALED

Eu·rope (yür´-əp), *n. and adv.* a phrase depicting the person being spoken to as in a high or precarious position. *"I'd say **Europe** a creek without a paddle."*

eu·tha·na·sia (yü-thən-ā´-zhə), *n. and prep.* the teenage generation of the world's most populous continent. *"If the Chinese rulers get too oppressive, the **euthanasia** will rise up."*

events (i-vents´), *n. and v.* a male passionately expressing a strongly felt emotion or opinion. *"He gets mad, **events**, then he calms down."*

ev·i·dence (e´-və-dens), *v. and adj.* being in possession of something compactly heavy; or being contractually connected to a person of low intelligence. *"We coulda got off if we didn't **evidence** lawyer."*

ex·haled (eks-hāld´), *n. and v.* a former spouse having kept a thing or person in a sustained position, either literally or figuratively. *"My **exhaled** my kids over my head for more alimony."*

ex·pend (eks-spend´), *n. and v.* one's former spouse on a buying spree. *"Dang! You should see my **expend** money."*

ex·tinct (ek-stinkt´), *n. and v.* the olfactory unpleasantness of one's former spouse. *"My new wife smells okay, but my **extinct** real bad."*

eye·lash (ī-lash´), *n. and v.* acting with aggression toward another. *"I feel bad when **eyelash** out at my wife."*

eye·sore (ī-sȯr´), *n. and v.* a first-person declaration of a visual perception. *"Back off, man, **eyesore** first!"*

Ff

fac·to·ry (fakt´-ər-ē), *n. and conj.* a truth or actuality considered as a precondition of a male person's actions. *"He knew it was a **factory** wouldn't've said it."*

EXTINCT

FANTASY

fad·ed (fād´-əd), *n. and v.* one's declaration of personal contempt. *"**Faded** that dude in the acid-wash jeans since I first met him."*

fair·ways (fer´-wāz), *conj. and n.* an opined conjecture concerning possible outcomes. *"**Fairways** to get in trouble, Tommy and the boys'll find them."*

fairy (fer´-ē), *adj. and n.* a description for a male person of light complexion and pigmentation. *"Jim's so **fairy** gets sunburned as soon as he goes outside."*

fan·ta·sy (fan´-tə-sē), *n. and v.* future tense for an enthusiastic supporter perceiving visually. *"For that **fantasy** the game, you're gonna have to take your hat off."*

fart (färt), *adv. and n.* a great distance, in relation to a thing. *"My old dog will still chase a stick, but it depends how **fart** goes."*

fat (fat´), *conj. and pron.* to identify, with condition or supposition. *"**Fat** ain't John Goodman, it must be his twin."*

fa·vor·ite (fā´-vər-it), *v. and n.* to give preferential treatment to a thing. *"My uncle hurt his knee in the war and now he tends to **favorite** when he walks."*

fea·si·ble (fēz´-ə-búl), *conj. and n.* the conditional identification of an uncastrated male bovine. *"**Feasible**, then I'm a cow."*

fe·ces (fē´-sēz), *conj. and v.* a conditional expression involving concern about being witnessed or discovered, often involving an illicit activity. *"**Feces** us together, the you-know-what is gonna hit the fan."*

feed (fēd´), *conj. and n.* the conditional desire for a male to act. *"I'd kick his butt, **feed** just step outside."*

FEEL

feel (fēl´), *conj. and n.* the conditional future action of a male person or animal. *"Will you ask this kind gentleman **feel** take his hands off my throat before I die?"*

fe·line (fē´-līn), *conj. and v.* a phrase implying action conditional on the untruthfulness of a male person. *"**Feline** to me, I'll scratch his eyes out."*

fe·males (fē´-mālz), *conj. and v.* a phrase implying action conditional on a male person putting a package or missive into the postal system, with the purpose of its delivery to an indicated address. *"**Females** it today, we should have it by Friday."*

Fer·ris wheel (fer´-əs-wēl´), *adj., n., and v.* equitable treatment or judgment, as applied to a group. *"The pitcher's daddy is the umpire, so I reckon that last call is as **Ferris wheel** get."*

fer·tile (fər´-til), *n. and conj.* the dense, hairy coat of an animal, up to a certain point in time. *"That dog done scratched his **fertile** it bled."*

FERRIS WHEEL

fe·tus (fēt´-əs), *v. and n.* to provide for group mastication. *"I wonder what they're gonna **fetus** for lunch."*

feud (fyüd´), *conj. and v.* involving any supposition concerning the action of another person. *"I woulda never shot at you, **feud** never shot at me."*

fi·as·co (fē-as´-gō), *conj., n., and v.* regarding an outcome conditional on the deterioration of the buttocks. *"She looks okay now, but **fiasco**, we're through."*

fid·dle (fid´-əl), *conj. and v.* regarding speculation on the result of an action about to be undertaken. *"I wonder **fiddle** get me all the way to the moon?"*

fil·i·greed (fil-ə-grēd´), *n. and v.* consent and acceptance by a person named Phillip. *"I said we should kick him out of the club, and **filigreed**."*

FIDDLE

FIRED

fire (fĭ´-ər), *conj. and v.* an empathetic supposition involving placing oneself in another's position. *"**Fire** you, I'd look for a new place to live."*

fired (fĭ´-ərd), *conj. and v.* interrogative about the correct aural perception of a meaning. *"**Fired** you right, you want me to give you my wallet?"*

fire·side (fĭr´-sīd), *conj. and n.* a phrase used to introduce the conditional action of a group in opposition to or competition with another. *"If your side wins, we wash your cars; **fireside** wins, you wash ours."*

fis·sion (fĭ´-shin), *n.* the act of capturing cold-blooded, aquatic craniate vertebrates. *"Ever since they put up that nuclear power plant, the **fission** been terrible."*

fis·sure (fĭsh´-ər), *n. and v.* regarding the actions of an aquatic creature. *"Ever since the earthquake, the **fissure** really bitin'."*

fist (fist´), *conj. and v.* the possible meaning of a state of being or of an action. *"**Fist** a first offense I'll let you go, but **fist** the second one, and **fist** for fightin', your butts are going to jail."*

fit·ness (fit´-nəs), *v. and n.* to be able to wear a snug garment. *"And you didn't think I could **fitness** bathin' suit after three kids!"*

fix·ture (fiks´-chür), *v.* to have repaired the property of another. *"It seems like you would be nicer to me since I just **fixture** car."*

fiz·zy (fiz´-ē), *prep., adj., and n.* concerning a male person and something belonging to him or intended to involve him. *"At my wedding my best man wore a tux, but **fizzy** wore his work clothes."*

fleet (flēt´), *conj. and v.* a phrase regarding the conditional future mastication of a male. *"We don't have enough food, so don't ask him **fleet** with us."*

FITNESS

Flor·i·da (flŏr´-ə-də), *n. and prep.* a room's lower plane, upon which everything else rests, or a place where elected officials assemble for the purpose of passing laws, with reference to the larger entity. *"In three years, no new bills got passed on the Florida senate."*

flu·id (flü´-əd), *n. and v.* the predicted effect of a viral sickness that causes fever, chills, sneezing, and a cough. *"My gramma's so dehydrated, if she caught the fluid kill her."*

fluo·res·cent (flŏr-es´-sint), *n. and v.* a negative declaration about the lowermost horizontal surface of a structure. *"You'd better mop it again, son. That fluorescent clean yet."*

fluo·ride (flŏr´-īd), *n. and v.* a hypothetical personal action concerning the lowest horizontal plane of a room. *"If that was my fluoride mop it."*

fly·er (flī´-ər), *n.* a blossoming reproductive shoot of a sporophytic organism. *"Let's swing by the cemetery so I can lay a flyer on Grandma's grave."*

FONDUE

fon·due (fän-dü´), *conj. and v.* involving uncertainty about a future action. *"I packed my own chute. I don't know **fondue** somethin' like that again."*

fore·close (för-klōz´), *prep. and n.* pertaining to a wardrobe acquisition. *"Marla said she needed money **foreclose**. What the hell's wrong with the dress she's got?"*

for·eign (för´-ən), *n. and prep.* anything done in an uninterrupted quadruplicate pattern. *"Them Montreal Canadiens are a good hockey team. They've won **foreign** a row."*

for·eign·er (för´-in-ər), *n. and prep.* an interior measurement of more than three but fewer than five persons or objects. *"Our town tried for the record for the most people in a telephone booth, but we could only get **foreigner**."*

FOREIGNER

FORTIFY

fore·skin (fôrs´-kin), *n. and v.* the possibilities available to an unseen but powerful strength or energy. *"If you come to my side, Luke Skywalker, then the foreskin be with you."*

for·ti·fy (fort´-əf-ī), *n. and conj.* concerning possible action toward an enclosed structure used for protection. *"I wouldn't attack that fortify was you."*

for·tu·itous (fôr-tü´-ət-əs), *prep. and n.* a declaration that a thing is intended for only a pair. *"Luckily, that sofa ain't so good for three people, but fortuitous."*

for·tunes (fôr´-chəns), *adj. and n.* the quadripartite region formed by the lower jaw of a particularly fleshy face. *"When Bill was just fat, he had two chins. But now that he's obese, he's got fortunes."*

fo·rum (fôr´-əm), *prep. and n.* concerning alliance with others. *"The thing about NASCAR drivers is there's no gray area. You're either forum or against 'em."*

FORTUNES

France (frants´), *prep. and n.* with regard to insects in the family Formicidae. *"We killed all the cockroaches and termites, but we gotta check **France**."*

fräu·lein (fröil´-īn), *prep. and n.* a phrase used in declaring one's ignorance. *"**Fräulein** know, she ran away because of you."*

free·dom (frē´-dəm), *adj. and n.* a triumvirate. *"Y'all better take a cookie now, 'cause dey's only **freedom** left."*

freeze (frēz´), *n. and v.* a declaration concerning the state of a male individual. *"**Freeze** a jolly good fellow!"*

freight (frāt´), *prep. and n.* with regard to a group of objects or units numbering twice as many as four. *"He's on a hunger strike . . . he hasn't eaten **freight** days."*

FREQUENT

fre·quent (frēk´-wənt), *n. and v.* the path of any person afflicted with grotesque physical oddities. *"Oh yeah, Officer, the **frequent** most definitely thataway."*

fuel (fyül´), *conj. and v.* a conditional request of an individual concerning their future action. *"**Fuel** stay, I'll fix you another drink."*

Gg

ga·la (gal´-ə), *n. and v.* a woman inclined to take action. *"Her sister might be a dud, but that **gala** show you a good time!"*

gal·lon (gal´-ən), *n. and prep.* a reference to the location of a female person. *"The one with the jug is ugly, but that **gallon** the horse ain't too bad."*

gar·den (gärd´-in), *n. and adv.* the bringing forth of a militia armed for the purposes of maintaining or restoring order. *"That riot was so bad they had to call the National **garden**."*

gar·ter (gärd´-ər), *v. and adj.* to protect or keep safe something belonging to a female. *"She eats with one arm in front of her plate to garter food."*

gas·tric (gas´-trik), *n.* a skillful act involving a flammable vaporous or liquid substance. *"Since he set his backside on fire, he don't do that gastric no more."*

Gem·i·ni (jem´-ən-ī), *n. and conj.* the speaker, as linked to a person with the given name James. *"Believe it or not, Gemini is identical twins."*

Geor·gia (jȯrj´-ə), *n. and adj.* a phrase connecting a person named George to a direct object. *"Dick Cheney shot him, but I'm sure they're gonna give old Georgia hard time about it."*

ger·min·ate (jər´-mən-āt), *n. and v.* a person of Saxon ancestry who has completed mastication. *"I served Hansel a ninety-eight-ounce steak, and that there germinate the whole thing."*

GASTRIC

GEYSER

ges·ture (jes´-chŭr), *adv. and adj.* pertaining to a prediction of compatibility. *"He's gesture kinda guy."*

gey·ser (gīz´-ər), *n. and v.* a judgment or declaration concerning a group of males. *"Those geyser idiots."*

glad·i·a·tor (glad´-ē-āt-ər), *adj. and v.* an exuberant reaction to the consumption of a female's cooking, by a male person. *"I'm gladiator muffins, or Grandma woulda been mad."*

god·dess (gäd´-əs), *n. and v.* the future action of a supreme being. *"Goddess gonna get you for that."*

gon·do·lier (gän-də-lir´), *v.* movement toward, with the purpose of gazing wantonly. *"Old Cooter's gondolier at the cheerleaders practicing."*

go·pher (gō´-fər), *v. and prep.* to move forth with a specific purpose. *"Man, I think I broke my leg in that damned rodent hole. You're gonna have to gopher help."*

gour·met (gȯr-mā´), *n. and v.* concerning the possible actions of anyone with the surname Gore. *"Holy cow, they're sayin' Al gourmet try and run for president again."*

gram·mar school (gra´-mə-skül´), *n.* an educational institution for female progenitors of mothers or fathers. *"Man, there must be some kind of grammar school teaches them all to yell like that."*

gran·di·ose (grand-ē-ōs´), *n. and v.* a male's obligation for one thousand dollars. *"It must be more than a grandiose those guys."*

gra·vy (grāv´-ē), *n. and pron.* concerning a male's reaction to or connection with a burial site. *"Soon as he gets near a gravy starts shakin'."*

GRAMMAR SCHOOL

GROCER

gro·cer (grōs´-ər), *adj. and conj.* an inquiry regarding the extent of repulsiveness. *"Is he grocer what?"*

gui·tar (gət-tär´), *v. and n.* to perform an errand resulting in the acquisition of a bituminous liquid. *"If we're gonna fix this roof we're gonna have to guitar."*

guz·zle (gəs´-əl), *n. and v.* the predicted action of a person who goes by a nickname for Gustav. *"Dave can knock back the bourbon, but guzzle drink you under the table."*

Hh

ham·let (ham´-lət), *n. and v.* salted, smoked pork and its effect or effects. *"The smell of frying hamlet everybody know that breakfast was ready."*

ham·per (ham´-pər), *n. and prep.* a cooked pig and its ratio to every member of a group. *"We gotta ration 'cause we only got one hamper man."*

hand·i·cap (han´-di-kap), *n.* a covering for the head that adds convenience in use. *"Work is way better now, thanks to my **handicap**!"*

har·dy (härd´-ē), *adv. and n.* a measure of force inflicted on a male. *"That boy got punched so **hardy** couldn't see straight."*

har·mo·ny (här´-mə-nē), *v. and n.* to cause damage to the speaker's mid-leg joint. *"If I don't pay them back by Tuesday, they're gonna **harmony**."*

hay·wire (hā´-wī-ər), *interj. and v.* to question the motivation for a current action. *"**Haywire** you flirtin' with my wife?"*

heal (hēl´), *n. and v.* to predict or suppose the future action of a specific male. *"If that surgeon keeps drinkin', **heal** kill somebody."*

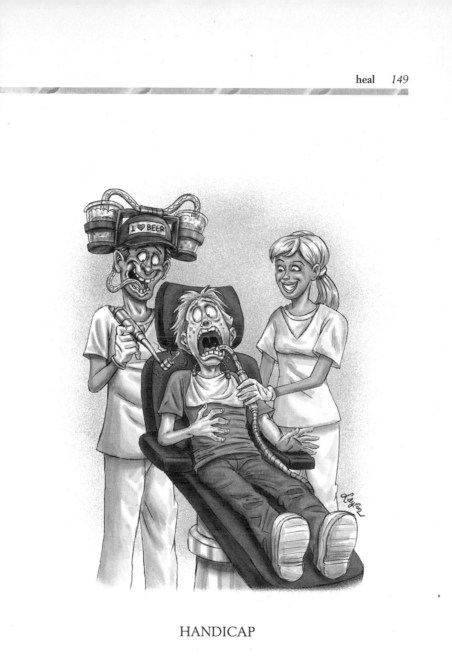

HANDICAP

healthy (hel´-thē), *n., conj., and pron.* the eternal damnation of a male person, dependent upon certain conditions. *"He's going to **healthy** don't change his ways."*

hea·then (hē´-thən), *n. and adv.* referring to the subsequent action of a male. *"After he said he was an atheist, **heathen** proceeded to take the Lord's name in vain."*

He·brews (hē´-brüz), *n. and v.* a statement concerning the ease with which a male will suffer a below-the-skin contusion. *"Don't be smackin' Timmy around like that, Cassie. **Hebrews** real easy."*

Heim·lich (hīm´-lik), *n. and v.* a person's declared intention to draw his or her tongue against a thing. *"After Mama gets through mixing the icing, **Heimlich** the spoon!"*

HERBIVORE

Hel·en (hel´-ən), *n. and conj.* the underworld, plus the aftermath. *"That poor guy's been to Helen back."*

he·lix (hē´-liks), *n. and v.* to drag the extended tongue along a person or object, as done by a male. *"It's below zero. If helix that fence his tongue is gonna get stuck."*

her·bi·cide (hər´-bə-sīd), *n. and adv.* a reference to the immediate surroundings of a woman. *"Sit herbicide the skinny guy so the boat don't tip over."*

her·bi·vore (hər´-bə-vȯr), *n. and conj.* concerning a female prior to an event. *"Unfortunately, he asked herbivore the accident."*

her·e·sy (her´-ə-sē), *n. and v.* the visual perception of a mass of filamentous epidermal outgrowth. *"Y'all better get me some Rogaine, what with all the heresy."*

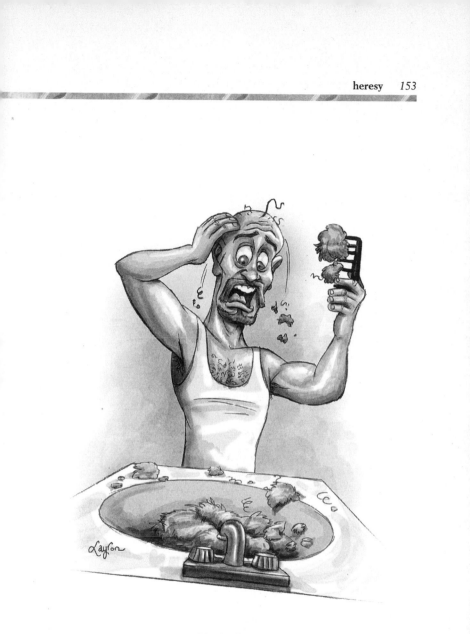

HERESY

HIGH-SPEED

he·roes (hē´-rōz), *n. and v.* a male person manually propelling a watercraft with oars. *"He oughta be fit, 'cuz **heroes** that boat for two hours every morning."*

her·o·in (her´-ə-win), *n. and v.* the predicted triumph of a long-eared mammal of the family Leporidae. *"You gotta be on drugs if you think a **heroin** a race against a tortoise."*

her·pes (hər´-pēz), *adj. and n.* small round vegetable seeds in the possession of a specific female. *"**Herpes** taste like they came out of a can."*

hide·away (hīd´-ə-wā), *n. and v.* the speaker's speculation on a future method or course of action. *"If **hideaway** to be a pro baseball player, I'd do it."*

high-speed (hī´-spēd), *n. and v.* the speaker when moving at a velocity beyond the posted limit. *"I drive slow when I see a cop, but if I don't see none, **high-speed**."*

HIPPIE

hill·side (hil-sīd´), *n. and v.* the predicted alliance of a male person. *"Don't ask her husband to back you . . . **hillside** with her every time."*

hip·pie (hip´-ē), *n.* a reference to the haunch of a specific male. *"Ever since he got shot in the **hippie** walks funny."*

His·pan·ic (his-pa´-nik), *adj. and n.* the hysterical reaction of a male. *"I'm worried about Dr. Hernandez, 'cause **Hispanic** attacks are gettin' more frequent."*

hoard (hòrd´), *v.* having committed an act of marital indiscretion, sometimes preceded by a financial interaction. *"She **hoard** around on him one too many times."*

Hol·land (häl´-ənd), *n. and conj.* half of a fairly popular pop duo from the late twentieth century. *"My favorite band is definitely **Holland** Oates."*

HISPANIC

hol·lan·daise (häl´-ən-dāz), *adj. and n.* a period of time in which one transported goods. *"I had a real sweet eighteen-wheeler back in my hollandaise."*

Hol·ly·wood (hȯl´-ē-wu̇d), *n., pron., and v.* speculation connecting an august institution or a part of a building to possible future action. *"Twenty bucks says if Pete Rose got into the Hollywood still bet on baseball."*

ho·ly (hōl´-ē), *n.* an indentation in the ground created by a specific male. *"That holy dug was deep."*

hon·es·ty (än´-əs-tē), *prep. and n.* into a position of rest upon a peg used in the opening play on any hole in the game of golf. *"If you want to drive all the way to the green, put your ball honesty."*

hon·or stu·dent (än´-ər stü´-dənt), *prep. and n.* for a female to be positioned over, and supported by, a pupil. *"Yeah, I knew piano lessons after midnight was weird, but I didn't suspect nothin' till I caught her honor student."*

Hoo·sier (hü´-zhər), *n. and v.* phrase used to inquire into another's relationship with someone. *"Hoosier daddy?"*

ho·ri·zon (hər-īz´-on), *n. and prep.* indicating a woman's focus on an object or her fervent desire, usually for something expensive. *"She's got horizon that mink coat."*

hor·net (hȯrn´-ət), *n. and pron.* a condition involving a brass instrument. *"Every night he plays that hornet keeps me up."*

horny (hȯrn´-ē), *n. and pron.* a phrase connecting a male to either a brass wind instrument or a protuberance of keratinized skin projecting outward from the skull of an animal. *"When he grabbed that bull by the horny got more than he'd bargained for."*

hor·ren·dous (hər-end´-əs), *n. and v.* any declaration concerning the backside of a female. *"She's got a pretty enough face, but horrendous huge and horrible."*

HORRENDOUS

HYSTERIA

hun·ger (həng´-ər), *v. and adj.* the suspending of a female's possession from a fixed object so that it does not touch the ground. *"We just about lost it when she **hunger** bra on the clothesline."*

hys·te·ria (hi-ster´-ē-ə), *n. and v.* a male person achieving intimidation using a concentrated and un-blinking ocular technique. *"Don't make eye contact with that dude—**hysteria** down."*

Ii

ice cream (īs´-krēm), *n. and v.* to cry out verbally in a loud, shrieking tone. *"Every time Junior wins a race, **ice cream** so loud the neighbors call the police."*

Ida·ho (īd´-ə-hō), *n. and v.* to have declared the possession of a tool used for breaking apart earth. *"**Idaho**, but Barry borrowed it, and I ain't seen it since."*

im·mi·grate (im´-ə-grāt), *n. and adj.* part of a phrase declaring a debt to a male. *"I owe **immigrate** deal of my success."*

im·pa·tience (im-pā´-shənts), *n.* any group
of impaired people confined to a place for healing.
"Impatience in the mental hospital scare me to death."

im·pede (im-pēd´), *n. and v.* a male having uri-
nated. *"Dangit, impede all over the fish I caught."*

im·plants (im-plants´), *adj. and n.* more than one
living multicellular organism that through photosyn-
thesis absorbs water and carbon dioxide and emits
oxygen. *"Implants are all saggy; they look like they
could use some water."*

in·cense (in´-sents), *conj. and n.* penny currency, in
addition to other moneys. *"Just tell me what it's gonna
cost me in dollars incense."*

in·cite (in-sīt´), *prep. and n.* indicating position
within a visual or achievable range. *"Always keep your
goals incite."*

IMPEDE

INNUENDO

In·dia (in´-dē-ə), *prep.* a function word indicating conditionality. *Flight attendant over the loudspeaker: "India 'vent of an emergency, your seat can be used as a toilet."*

in·fa·my (in´-fə-mē), *adv. and n.* another person's intent to exact physical punishment. *"Ever since I went on that crime spree, the cops have had it infamy."*

in·her·it (in-her´-ət), *n.* concerning the interior location of the speaker. *"I don't know about outside, but inherit stinks."*

in·no·cence (in´-o-sints), *prep., n., and adv.* a phrase describing a quality of or substance within a woman after a certain circumstance. *"She married that jerk, and I ain't seen a lick of happiness innocence."*

in·nu·en·do (in-yə-wen´-dō), *prep. and n.* indicating the passage of anything through a wall opening made of glass that can be opened or closed. *"Hey, dude, I just saw a bird fly innuendo."*

in·qui·ries (in-kwīr´-ēz), *prep. and n.* referring to the actions of a specific male member of a vocal group. *"That boy's a monster at home, but **inquiries** a saint."*

in·sid·i·ous (in-sid´-ē-əs), *adv., n., and v.* an action by or quality of a male, as an alternative to another action or quality. *"We thought he was loyal, but **insidious** stabbin' us in the back."*

in·stinct (in´-stinkt), *prep. and n.* concerning the level of olfactory offensiveness. *"I'll give it an 8 in sound, and a 10 **instinct**."*

in·tense (in-tents´), *prep. and n.* inside portable canvas shelters. *"Next time we go campin', I suggest we sleep **intense**."*

in·ter·cept (in-tər-sept´), *v. and conj.* concerning conditions placed on the permissibility of ingress. *"That there's the operatin' room. You can't **intercept** if you're a doctor."*

NATIONAL BURP
CHAMPIONSHIPS

INSTINCT

INTERESTING

in·ter·est·ing (in´-tə-res-ting), *prep. and n.* having a preference for relaxation. *"Bob said he was a good pilot, but now I see he's more **interesting**."*

in·ter·face (in-tər-fās´), *prep. and n.* to a position of contact with the front part of a female's head. *"That guy hit a fastball and it flew right **interface**!"*

in·ter·view (in-tər-vyü´), *prep. and n.* entering a position that allows visual perception. *"Just shoot as soon as it comes **interview**!"*

In·u·it (in´-yü-ət), *conj. and n.* a pronouncement that another is to be the targeted object, usually within the context of a game. *"We're playing tag, **Inuit**."*

in·un·dat·ed (in´-ən-dāt-əd), *prep. and v.* to have entered and commenced courtship. *"That snake snuck **inundated** my girl when I was out of town."*

in·ward (in´-wərd), *prep. and n.* concerning the record of a person's verbalizations. *"A scout is trustworthy inward and deed."*

io·ta (ī-ōt´-ə), *n. and v.* first-person form of admitting debt. *"Sure I shot him, Officer, but in my defense, iota lotta money to that guy."*

iPod (ī´-päd), *n. and v.* a personal reference to having groped or roughly handled another person or an object. *"iPod her for about twenty minutes before I realized she was my mother-in-law."*

Iraq; Iran (i-rak´; i-ran´), *n.; v.* the ampleness of one's bosom; to compete for. *"If I had Iraq like hers, I'd Iran for Miss Tennessee, too."*

iron (ī´-ərn), *n. and v.* a personal proclamation about the currency one receives in exchange for the services one renders. *"Workin' down in the mine, iron twenty-three bucks an hour."*

IRAQ; IRAN

is·land (ī´-lənd), *n. and v.* to declare one's projected arrival. *"The plane takes off at two and island at seven."*

is·land·er (ī´-lənd-ər), *n. and v.* to temporarily give to a female. *"If islander any more money, I'll be broke."*

iso·late (ī-sə-lāt´), *n. and v.* an explanation for extreme tardiness, usually in the form of an excuse. *"Sorry isolate, but I hit a deer on the way over here!"*

is·sue (ish-ü´), *n. and v.* concerning an ultimatum to another. *"Somebody's gotta go through that door first. Either issue or me, brother."*

Jj

jack·et (ja´-kət), *v. and n.* to raise a specified object on a sturdy portable device, using leverage. *"You can't change the tires until you jacket up."*

JAMAICAN

JESTER

Ja·kar·ta (jə-kär´-tə), *n. and prep.* pertaining to a person's automobile. *"Oh yeah, that mechanic at Tom's garage'll get Jakarta run real good."*

Ja·mai·can (jə-māk´-ən), *n. and v.* an inquiry concerning another's creation. *"Hey there, Jimmy, what Jamaican for the science fair?"*

jest·er (jest´-ər), *adv. and n.* exclusive indication of a person who is connected to the one being spoken to. *"I'm not letting all y'all in, jester friend in the glasses."*

jour·nal (jər´-nol), *n. and v.* a proclamation excluding the person being addressed from a group. *"Don't make fun of me, Al . . . journal Einstein yourself!"*

jour·ney (jər´-nē), *n.* a specified person's mid-leg joint. *"You hurt journey in that fight?"*

JOURNAL

ju·di·cious (jü-dish´-əs), *n. and v.* interrogative regarding whether the person being addressed spoke critically of the speaker and his or her associates. *"Sorry I called you a gossip, but didn't judicious a while back?"*

juic·er (jü´-sər), *pron. and n.* the start of an ironic pronouncement addressed to a male person of authority or distinction. *"I knew Jack Kennedy, and juicer are no Jack Kennedy."*

juic·i·er (joo´-sē-ər), *n. and v.* an inquiry concerning whether another has perceived, visually, a female; often involves the disrobed state of the subject. *"Juicier nekkid?"*

Ju·ly (jü-lī´), *n. and v.* interrogative regarding another's veracity. *"Why July about it?"*

junc·tion (jənk´-shən), *n. and v.* a phrase assessing the state of debris in a negative way. *"That junction be left at the dump, stupid!"*

junc·ture (jənk´-chŭr), *n. and adv.* a declaration of certainty pertaining to rubbish. *"You're throwin' it all out, but this juncture looks good to me."*

junk·ies (jənk´-ēz), *n. and v.* a phrase connecting useless or discarded articles to the actions of a male person. *"Don't buy any of that junkies sellin', 'cuz he'll only use the money to buy drugs."*

Ju·pi·ter (jü´-pə-tər), *n. and v.* imperative regarding another's action, with an implied threat or warning. *"Jupiter stop jumpin' on the bed."*

jus·tice (jəs´-təs), *adv.* comparatively equal. *"That lawyer's case is justice good as the other guy's."*

KATMANDU

Kat·man·du (kat-man´-dü), *n. and v.* a mythical character with feline qualities and his actions or function. *"I get why we let Aquaman into the club, but what the hell's the **Katmandu**?"*

Ken·ya (ken´-yə), *v. and n.* to inquire as to the abilities of another. *"Hey, Rudy, **Kenya** hand me a beer?"*

Khar·toum (kär-tüm´), *n. and prep.* a phrase connecting an automobile with a male person. *"Paul's been actin' all high and mighty since Pa died and left the **Khartoum**."*

kilo·watt (kil´-ə-wät), *v. and n.* interrogative as to the specific identity of an intended prey animal, with the objective of ending its life. *"Tell me one more time: we're goin' out to **kilowatt**?"*

KILOWATT

kilt (kilt´), *v.* having caused a living thing to expire. *"If he was my husband, I'd have **kilt** him a long time ago."*

kil·ter (kilt´-ər), *v. and n.* to end the life of a female. *"Betty drank so much gin last night, it coulda **kilter**."*

klep·to·ma·ni·ac (klep-tə-mā´-nē-ak), *v. and n.* to have collided with a person suffering from severe mental illness. *"When I was drivin' down by the nuthouse the other day, I think I mighta **kleptomaniac**."*

knock·er (näk´-ər), *v. and n.* to disparage a female. *"Don't **knocker** till you tried her."*

Ku·wait (kü-wāt´), *v.* indicating the ability to employ patience. *"I'm really hungry now, but I guess I **Kuwait**."*

KLEPTOMANIAC

LAMINATE

Ll

lac·quer thin·ner (lak´-ər thin´-ər), *v. and adv.* to prefer less corporeal mass on a female. *"I still think Kirstie Alley's cute, but I lacquer thinner."*

la·dle (lā´-dil), *v. and conj.* at rest or repose up to a mentioned time or event. *"Just let it ladle everybody cools off a bit."*

lam·i·nate (lam´-en-āt), *n. and v.* a young sheep, in relation to something it is not. *"I ordered the laminate cooked the way I wanted it."*

lar·i·at (ler´-ē-ət), *n. and prep.* interrogative regarding the location of a person named Laurence. *"Where's lariat?"*

la·ser (lāz´-ər), *v. and adj.* a female's setting down of something. *"As soon as she laser big butt down for a nap, we're leaving."*

lawn (lȯn´), *n.* a reference to the rules of a society; often used in connection with a popular television show. *"You catch that episode of* **Lawn** Order *last night?"*

left field (left-fēld´), *n. and v.* an object located on the opposite of the right side, and the tactile sensation it elicited. *"I don't know, man, her* **left field** *way bigger than her right."*

less·er (les´-ər), *conj. and adj.* except if, as pertaining to a female. *"***Lesser** *mom changes her mind, I don't think we're going out tonight."*

let·ter car·ri·er (let´-ər-ka´-rē-ər), *v. and n.* to suggest that a woman transport her personal belongings herself. *"If she wants to bring all that junk,* **letter carrier** *own luggage."*

LETTER CARRIER

LICENSE

let·ter·head (let´-ər-hed), *v. and n.* a suggested action concerning a certain female's cranial region. *"No worries, man, she's in here drunk every night—just letterhead hit the bar."*

let·tuce (let´-əs), *v. and n.* to suggest allowance of a specified action by a group. *"Oh Lord, I swear I will never play chicken again if You just please lettuce survive this!"*

Le·vi (lēv´-ī), *v. and n.* a phrase connecting the act of departure to the speaker. *"If I Levi ain't coming back."*

li·ar (lī´-ər), *v. and adj.* to set or put down something of a female's. *"I don't care if she's cheating on me, she can liar head on my pillow anytime."*

li·cense (lī-sints´), *n. and adv.* a reference to the most recent instance of fibbing. *"She ran over me with the pickup three days ago, and I ain't told a license."*

li·chen (līˊ-kən), *n. and v.* the result of an untruth. *"I don't care how long you been married, one big lichen wreck it all."*

Li·ma (lēˊ-mə), *v. and adj.* to demand that another abandon something or someone possessed or claimed by one. *"Lima girl alone!"*

liv·er (livˊ-ər), *v. and conj.* regarding options other than earthly existence. *"I'm so depressed I don't care if I liver die."*

lu·nar (lünˊ-ər), *n. and conj.* a person afflicted with mental instability and a possible alternative. *"Is Betty a lunar what?"*

lu·rid (lùrˊ-əd), *n. and v.* a conjecture about an object intended to decoy or tempt. *"I'd be shocked if that lurid catch fish."*

LUNAR

Tanya

Madge

MAGISTRATE

ma·chete (mə-shed´-ē), *adj. and n.* the speaker's freestanding storage structure as acted upon by a male. *"It weren't machete knocked down, it was my neighbor's."*

mag·is·trate (ma´-jə-strāt), *n. and v.* declaration concerning the heterosexual orientation of a woman named Madge. *"Tanya's gay, but magistrate."*

maid·en (mād´-in), *v. and prep.* indicating the place of manufacture or creation of something. *"Seems like everything these days is maiden China."*

ma·jor (mā´-jər), *v. and n.* a phrase proclaiming that the person being spoken to has been forced or induced to do something. *"Ha ha, major look!"*

man·da·rin (man´-də-rən), *interj. and n.* emphatically expressed concern about the state of two or more people. *"Lee and Bobby Chang just got back from Vegas, and **mandarin** a bad mood."*

Man·hat·tan (man-ha´-tən), *interj. and v.* advice for action. *"**Manhattan** you better get outta here? You just hit that dude's car."*

man·i·cure (man´-ə-kyür), *n. and v.* an adult male person offered as relief for the symptoms of a disease or condition. *"If you're feeling frisky a good **manicure** you."*

man·i·fes·to (man-əf-əs´-tō), *interj. and n.* an expression of despair concerning a final chance, as for repair. *"**Manifesto** do it, I don't know what will."*

man·i·fold (man´-əf-ōld), *interj. and adj.* colloquial; expressing the possible future actions of an elderly person. *"**Manifold** Mike hadn't a fallen into the bear trap, he'd be with us today."*

MANNEQUIN

man·ne·quin (man´-i-kən), *n. and v.* regarding the abilities of a male person. *"Ain't a **mannequin** take my bear in a fight."*

man·sion (man´-shən), *n. and v.* a phrase used to warn about the negative repercussions of a male person's actions. *"That **mansion** be doin' that."*

man·tle (man´-təl), *n. and prep.* a male, up to a certain point in time. *"It's amazing, but that chick used to be a **mantle** she got that operation."*

man·u·script (man´-yə-skript), *interj. and n.* regarding another's written document, usually intended for dramatic performance. *"**Manuscript** was real good! Once I started readin' it I couldn't put it down!"*

ma·ple (mā´-pəl), *v. aux. and v.* expressing the possibility of the act of yanking. *"Timmy's adorable, but he **maple** your hair out."*

MAPLE

march (märch´), *adj. and n.* a curved structure, as of a ceiling or instep, belonging to the speaker. *"The podiatrist said my left foot is flat, so if I wanna be in the parade, I'll need better support for **march**."*

mar·ga·rine (märj´-ər-ən), *n. and v.* a reference to the current location or situation of any woman named Marge, along with her companion or companions. *"Yup . . . Bob just took off, and I could be wrong, but I think me and **margarine** big trouble."*

mar·ket (märk´-ət), *v. and n.* to note something in writing. *"I'm getting married on March first, so make sure to **market** on your calendar."*

mar·ma·lade (mär´-mə-lād), *n. and v.* a female progenitor assuming a prone position. *"It was a sad story. His **marmalade** down one day and just never got up again."*

MARGARINE

MARSUPIAL

mar·shal (märsh´-əl), *n. and v.* a prediction concerning the future state of a wetland. *"That marshal swallow your tractor right up."*

mar·su·pi·al (mär-süp´-ē-əl), *adj. and n.* a phrase suggesting an expected result of a male's ingestion of any additional quantity of a liquid food made with cooked meats or vegetables. *"If he eats any marsupial explode."*

mas·cara (mas-ker´-ə), *v.* to assume affection for. *"I don't know if you realize it, Bill, but Jenny mascara lot for you."*

mas·cot (mas´-kät), *n. and v.* indicating the condition or state of the Christian Eucharist. *"When old lady Watkins took a swing at the organist, I'd say that's right about when mascot out of hand."*

mas·och·ist (mas´-əu-kist), *n. and v.* the act of pressing one's lips against a person or object in relation to the celebration of the Christian Eucharist. *"I'm sure I'll suffer for it later, but during the first masochist the widow Johnson, and during the second masochist her sister."*

MASCOT

mass (mas´), *adj. and n.* one's own backside. *"I've got to go on a diet. **Mass** is the size of a barn."*

mat·a·dor (mat´-ə-dȯr), *n., v., and n.* a phrase declaring one's proximity to a swinging or sliding barrier used to bar or allow passage into or out of a structure or between rooms. *"**Matador,** man, but it's locked."*

mate (māt´), *n. and v.* a declaration that one has surpassed seven but not yet reached nine years of existence. *"When they asked me how old I was, I said **mate**."*

May·ber·ry (mā´-ber-ē), *v.* a possible option pertaining to the entombment of someone or something. *"They **Mayberry** her next to her mother."*

may·hem (mā´-hem), *v. aux. and v.* the possibility of, through the act of sewing, altering an article of clothing so as to shorten it or neaten its edge. *"These pants are a little long, so I **mayhem** 'em."*

MAYOR

may·or (mā´-yər), *v. and adj.* a term expressing a possibility associated with the person being addressed. *"Here's to you, Jenny . . . mayor problems be few, now that your mother, that witch, is dead and gone!"*

mean (mēn), *pron. and conj.* the speaker plus someone related to a female. *"Mean her sister wandered off behind the barn for a while."*

me·an·der (mē´-and-ər), *n.* a reference to one's self and a female. *"I would have gone out with Lucy, but meander cousin was already datin'."*

me·di·ate (mēd´-ē-ət), *n. and v.* animal flesh consumed by an individual male. *"No wonder his stomach burst, considerin' the amount of mediate."*

mel·a·no·ma (mel-ə-nō´-mə), *n. and v.* to profess knowledge of something, such as another's feelings or intentions, when speaking to a person named Melvin. *"Melanoma mole looks funny, but I'm going to the tanning parlor anyway."*

men·stru·ate (men´-strāt), *n. and adj.* adult males gaining through understanding. *"About once a month my wife acts like she's got to set all* **menstruate** *about somethin'."*

men·tion (men´-shən), *n. and v.* the start of a proclamation expressing a desired restriction on male behavior. *"**Mention** wear skirts, unless they're Scottish."*

menu (men´-yü), *n. and pron.* adult human males in relation to the person being addressed. *"Wolfgang Puck is one of the richest **menu** would ever want to meet."*

midg·et (mi´-jət), *adj. and n.* a term regarding one's relation who is inflicted with mental deficiencies. *"**Midget** brother just drowned my truck."*

min·i·a·ture (min´-ə-chŭr), *n., prep., and adj.* more than one adult male person in a particular position or relation to the person being addressed. *"I thought you said there was gonna be a lot of hot **miniature** party."*

MINIATURE

MISTAKE

min·is·ter (min´-ə-stər), *n. and v.* the speaker's avowal to personally create agitation. *"If that preacher shows up here tonight, minister up a whole lot of trouble."*

min·is·try (min´-əs-trē), *n. and v.* a declaration that one is located in the upper parts of a woody perennial plant with an elongated single stem. *"Look up, Reverend, ministry!"*

mi·sog·y·ny (mə-säj´-en-ē), *n. and conj.* the act of kneading muscles in order to relieve tension, as linked to a male. *"He was gettin' a misogyny fell asleep halfway through."*

mis·take (mis-tāk´), *n. and v.* to command an unmarried female person to seize or capture something. *"Please, mistake the picture!"*

mis·trust (mis-trəst´), *n. and v.* an appeal to convince a female of one's honesty or reliability. *"Mistrust me on this one. I can fix your car."*

mi·to·sis (mī-tōs´-əs), *n. and v.* the state of the digits of one's foot. *"After all that walkin', mitosis sore."*

mix·ture (miks´-chər), *v. and adj.* to have combined or melded two or more substances, at least one of them belonging to the person being addressed. *"You mixture chocolate in my peanut butter."*

moan (mōn´), *n. and v.* to declare one's intentions. *"I don't care how big her old man is, moan ask her out."*

mob·ster (mäb´-stər), *n. and v.* an unruly crowd causing a disruption. *"Once they started drinkin', I saw that mobster up a pack of trouble."*

mo·dem (mōd´-əm), *v. and n.* to have cut or thrashed with a bladed machine. *"I thought about burnin' my front yard and my backyard, but I just modem instead."*

MIXTURE

MONOLOGUE

mol·li·fy (mäl´-əf-ī), *n. and conj.* concerning permission to proceed to a large indoor shopping complex, under certain promised conditions. *Teen girl on phone: "My mom says I can go to the **mollify** finish all my homework."*

mon·i·tor (män´-ət-ər), *n., v., and conj.* a declaration as to two alternatives for one's placement. *"They already picked the team, Steve . . . either **monitor** not."*

mon·key (mən´-kē), *adj. and n.* the speaker's ownership of an instrument that provides access to a locked place. *"I can go to the zoo whenever I like—I got **monkey**."*

mono·logue (män´-ə-lȯg), *v. and n.* a declaration of one's position on a portion of cut timber. *"Please tell me I **monologue**."*

mono·rail (män´-ə-rāl), *n., v., and adv.* stating the authenticity or intensity of one's current state. *"No way am I folding now, baby, **monorail** streak."*

MONORAIL

mon·soon (män´-sün), *n., v., and adv.* the speaker's proclamation that in a short period of time he or she will be expected to proceed to a stage, usually to perform entertainment. *"I'm sure you could give me a few pointers on my jokes, dude, but I don't have the time, 'cuz monsoon."*

mor·al (mȯr´-əl), *adv. and conj.* to a greater extent, with the possibility of an alternative. *"I've been to that strip club a hundred times, moral less."*

mor·bid (mȯr´-bid), *adj. and n.* another offer. *"One morbid like that and this auction's closed!"*

mo·ron (mȯr´-än), *n. and prep.* the addition of a greater quantity to that already present. *"I told him that I already put hot sauce on the pizza, but the idiot just kept pourin' moron."*

Mos·cow (mäs´-kaů), *adj. and n.* a female bovine owned by the speaker's female parent. *"Dad's new wife is gonna have a fit if we don't get Moscow outta his barn."*

MOTHER

mo·tel (mō-tel´), *v.* to threaten to verbally reveal forbidden activity. *"If you don't stop peein' in the pool, I motel Daddy!"*

moth·er (mə´-thər), *adj.* remaining or additional, particularly as possessed by or in relation to an individual. *"My oldest brother is all right, but mother brother's crazy."*

mo·to·cross (mōt´-ō-krȯs), *n. and prep.* a water-filled trench used around a structure to prevent access from one side to the other. *"If your home is a castle, you should put a motocross your whole yard."*

mov·ies (müv´-ēz), *v. and n.* a phrase connecting a male to a change of position. *"If he doesn't movies in big trouble."*

mud·dle (məd´-əl), *n. and v.* a prediction concerning sodden or soaked earth. *"Soak them pants, boy, or that muddle never come out."*

mul·let (məl´-ət), *v. and n.* to ponder a decision. *"Do I want a crew cut or a bowl cut? Hmmm. Lemme **mullet** over."*

mum·mi·fy (məm´-if-ī), *n. and conj.* a conditional phrase connecting the speaker to the female who gave birth to him or her. *"I'll hafta ask my **mummify** can play with that weird Egyptian kid."*

mus·ket (məs´-kət), *v.* to declare a personal promise for future action. *"I **musket** my butt outta this bed and find a job . . . tomorrow."*

mus·tache (məs´-stash), *v.* to urge secretive storage. *"Our collective band of ne'er-do-wells **mustache** our ill-gotten gains in a suitable hiding spot to keep the authorities from discerning their whereabouts, what ho?"*

mu·ti·neer (myüt-ən-ir´), *n. and prep.* the presence, at a particular place, of a person who is unable to speak. *"You better fetch a pen and paper if you want any answers—there's a **mutineer**."*

MYSTIFY

mys·ti·fy (mist´-əf-ī), *v. and conj.* a preamble to an excuse for having failed to hit or strike successfully. *"I wouldn't've mystify hadn't've been so drunk."*

Nn

na·ked (nā´-kəd), *n. and v.* a declaration of the capability of others. *"I'll do what I want, an' naked do what they want."*

nap·kin (nap´-kən), *n. and v.* a negotiation presuming a doze; commonly used by children. *"If I take a napkin I go?"*

nar·row (na´-rō), *conj. and n.* in addition to a shafted projectile with a pointed or sharpened end. *"Sure wish I hadn't bought Kenny that bow narrow."*

na·sal (nāz´-əl), *n. and v.* a phrase used to express an opinion or observation about a group as a whole. *"See them guys? Nasal a bunch of jerks."*

NARROW

nav·i·gate (nav´-ə-gāt), *v. and n.* to lack possession of a closable, usually hinged barrier. *"I drove through the fence 'cause the dang fool did **navigate**."*

nee·dle (nēd´-əl), *v.* to desire urgently. *"After I finish this, I'm gonna **needle** little vacation."*

ne·gate (ni-gāt´), *n.* a swinging barricade. *"Open **negate** and let me in!"*

net·works (net´-wərkz), *n. and v.* the functioning of a woven trap. *"We'll catch a lot of fish if this **networks**."*

neu·ter (nü´-tər), *adv. and prep.* unfamiliar with. *"I'm **neuter** town, so I get lost a lot."*

NEEDLE

NEVADA

Ne·va·da (nə-va´-də), *adv. and v.* to not ever have possessed. *"Believe it or not, I Nevada girl to call my own."*

New Hamp·shire (nü-ham´-shər), *n. and adv.* a confident declaration concerning the edible parts of a fresh pig. *"That old leftover ham made everybody sick, but this New Hampshire does taste good."*

nin·com·poop (nin´-kəm-püp), *adv. and v.* to subsequently move toward and defecate. *"He barks all day, nincompoop on my lawn at night!"*

No·ah (nō´-ə), *v.* to have acquaintance or comprehension of. *"Anyone Noah guy with a boat we could use?"*

no·ble (nō´-bul), *adj. and n.* completely without prevarication. *"That tree jumped right out in front of me, Judge, noble."*

no·bler (nō´-blər), *adj. and n.* without any obscuring smear or indistinctness. *"Ain't had **nobler** in my vision since I got laser surgery."*

noc·turne (näkt´-ərn), *v. and n.* to have impregnated at least two females. *"I think I mighta **nocturne** her sister up!"*

no·el (nō-el´), *adj. and n.* the absence of a pit that supplies water. *"Hell no, I didn't see **noel** until I fell into it."*

noo·dle (nü´-dəl), *adj. and conj.* in pristine condition, and the termination of that status. *"My truck was brand-**noodle** I drove it into that tree."*

nosy (nō´-zē), *v. and n.* to cognitively understand something regarding a male. *"I don't mean to be a buttinsky here, but am I the only guy who **nosy** cain't swim?"*

NOCTURNE

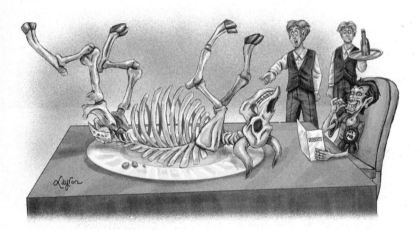

OBLIVIATE

no·ti·fied (nōt´-əf-īd), *v. and conj.* to claim under-standing, conditionally; often used as an excuse to cover ignorance. *"I woulda **notified** been told."*

nui·sance (nü´-sints), *adj. and adv.* pertaining to the duration of an object's existence. *"Old Tom's gun ain't been **nuisance** 1962."*

nurse·maid (nərs´-mād), *n. and v.* caused by a caregiver to the ill. *"She's so hot, that **nursemaid** my blood pressure go up."*

obliv·i·ate (ä-bliv´-ē-āt), *n. and v.* a declaration of a confident conviction concerning the history of an-other's mastication. *"**Obliviate** the whole thing."*

ob·long (ä´-blȯng), *n. and v.* a statement concern-ing the speaker's feeling of being comfortably, or un-comfortably, located. *"I need to get back down south. This is not where **oblong**."*

odor (ō´-dər), *adj.* a comparative term describing the advanced existence of a thing or person. *"She's odor than dirt."*

od·ys·sey (ä´-də-sē), *v.* to suggest the duty or obligation of another to notice a particular thing. *"You odyssey the rack on her sister."*

of·fense (ə-fens´), *n.* a barricade. *"No offense, ma'am, but I'm putting up offense."*

of·fice (äf´-fəs), *prep. and adj.* a phrase stating that a male no longer occupies nor is in possession of something that belongs to him. *"If he thinks I'm working on Super Bowl Sunday, he's office rocker."*

of·fi·cial (ə-fish´-əl), *n. and v.* a prediction concerning the future of an aquatic craniate vertebrate. *"Everybody knows official taste better if you squeeze a little lemon on after you cook it."*

OFFICIAL

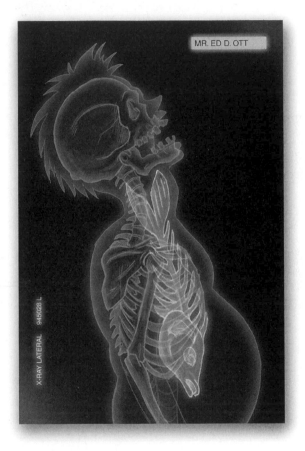

OFFICIATE

of·fi·ci·ate (ə-fish´-ē-āt), *n. and v.* an aquatic animal consumed by a male. *"I'm guessing Pete choked—musta been **officiate**."*

ol·fac·to·ry (äl-fak´-tə-rē), *adj. and n.* an aging manufacturing facility. *"They're closin' down the **olfactory** on account of it smells so bad."*

ol·ive (ä´-liv), *n. and v.* to proclaim one's existence, especially as under certain circumstances. *"I'll never drink another martini if **olive** to be a hundred."*

om·e·let (äm´-lət), *n. and v.* to allow another a thing or action. *"If you apologize, **omelet** you outta here alive."*

on·line (ȯn-līn´), *adv. and v.* to continue telling an untruth. *"I saw you lookin' at Internet porn, so don't go **online** to me about it."*

onus (ōn´-əs), *v. and n.* to be in the possession or control of other persons. *"We just work here. He don't* **onus."**

Ophe·lia (ə-fēl´-yə), *n. and v.* used to declare empathy for another's physical or spiritual discomfort. *"**Ophelia** pain."*

op·pose (əp´-ōz), *prep. and n.* into an elevated position on more than one thing. *"Let's climb **oppose** trees."*

op·press (ə-pres´), *n. and v.* one's application of steady, bodily force. *"So you're tellin' me if **oppress** that button, this little old room we're in is gonna slide up the side of the building?!"*

oral (ȯr´-əl), *conj. and n.* an alternative scenario, usually promising an unpleasant action. *"Listen up, boy. You better clean your room good **oral** ground you for a week."*

OPPRESS

ORDEAL

or·ange (är´-inj), *v. and adv.* a contraction of "are not"; usually used as an interrogative. *"**Orange** you glad I didn't drive drunk?"*

or·deal (òr-dēl´), *conj. and v.* a phrase connecting something to an alternative involving the act of distribution. *"Quit the game **ordeal** the cards!"*

Or·eos (òr´-ē-ōz), *n. and v.* a male person's obligations, under certain circumstances. *"Either he brings back my lawn mower, **Oreos** me two hundred dollars!"*

ori·ga·mi (òr-ə-gä´-mē), *conj. and v.* a phrase connecting something to an alternative involving something possessed by the speaker. *"I could use this, **origami** a twelve-gauge in the cab."*

or·i·gin (òr´-ə-jən), *conj. and n.* involving a choice between any item and a colorless alcoholic beverage made from distilled grain spirits flavored with juniper berries. *"Hmmm . . . should I have a blueberry daiquiri **origin** fizz?"*

os·trich (ä´-strich), *n. and v.* one engaging in the act of muscular elongation. *"I'll be there soon as **ostrich** my legs."*

out·line (aút´-līn), *adv. and v.* to be publicly relaying untruthful statements. *"My ex-husband been **out-line** about what I did."*

out·stand·ing (aút-stan´-ding), *adv. and v.* assuming an erect posture in a place away from the interior of an inhabitable structure. *"That moron's **outstanding** in the middle of the street."*

overt (ō-vərt´), *adv. and n.* above or across a thing. *"We tried to drive **overt**, but we got stuck."*

owl (aú´-əl), *adv. and v.* interrogative addressing future means. *"**Owl** we get in if we ain't got keys?"*

OVERT

ox·en (äks´-ən), *n. and prep.* a domesticated bovine, encased or enclosed. *"If we put that boy* Bos taurus *with that girl* Bos taurus, *pretty soon we'll have a baby* **oxen** *here."*

Pa·cif·ic (pə-si´-fik), *adj.* exact; in precise detail. *"He asked if I'd ever shot anyone, and I asked him if he could be more* **Pacific**.*"*

pac·i·fy (pas´-əf-ī), *v. and conj.* during a contest, to overtake a competitor, under certain conditions. *"Dale Earnhardt was a fearless racer. He was like, 'I don't care what you do. I'll* **pacify** *feel like it.' "*

pad·dle (pad´-əl), *n. and v.* the predicted state of a residence. *"I've looked at many places, but this* **paddle** *be perfect."*

PARANOIA

pal·ace (pal´-əs), *n. and conj.* an ally compared to something else. *"The king is not as good a **palace** you think he is."*

pan·da (pan´-də), *n. and prep.* a metal container used for cooking, as connected to an action. *"That ain't the **panda** asked for, stupid!"*

para·chute (per´-ə-shüt), *n. and v.* two human beings and the prediction that they will cause a projectile to move at a high velocity. *"Watch out for Bonnie and Clyde, 'cuz that **parachute** ya just for fun."*

par·a·dise (per´-ə-dīs), *n.* two matched, numbered cubes for use for gaming. *"He thinks he's special since he got that fuzzy **paradise** hanging from his rearview mirror."*

par·a·lyze (per-ə-līz´), *n.* two untruths. *"She said I was ugly and fat. That's a **paralyze**! Well, actually, it's one lie. I'm not fat!"*

PARANORMAL

par·a·mount (per´-ə-maûnt), *n. and v.* two living beings and the prediction that they will climb atop. *"The most important thing to know about rabbits is that they're so frisky, a paramount one female."*

para·noia (per´-ə-nòi-ə), *n. and v.* two living beings engaging in irritating behavior. *"You can't let that paranoia."*

para·nor·mal (par-ə-nòr´-məl), *n. and adj.* two things or persons representative of the mean or otherwise average. *"Don't pay any attention to them, Jane, I think you've got a paranormal kids."*

Par·is (par´-əs), *n. and v.* used to express or describe the state of being of a set of two things. *"That salesman told me these French shoes were comfortable, but dang, this Paris killin' me."*

par·o·dy (per´-ə-dē), *n. and pron.* a phrase connecting two matched things or a single thing composed of two matched parts to a male. *"He wanted a pair of pants, but them ain't the parody wanted."*

PARODY

PASTEURIZE

par·ty (pärt´-ē), *n. and pron.* a phrase connecting one segment of a whole, as with a character in a performance, to a male. *"He was only wearing a dress 'cuz that was the party was tryin' out for."*

pas·teur·ize (pas´-chər-īz), *prep. and n.* moving beyond or to the other side of the ocular organs of the person addressed by the speaker. *"I don't know how you missed that duck, Dick ∴ . it flew right pasteurize."*

pas·tor (past´-ər), *adj. and conj.* a phrase connecting a time gone by to an alternative. *"All my wives, pastor present, have been preachers' daughters."*

pas·ture (pas´-chür), *adv.* traveling by something owned or occupied by another. *"Hey, Charla, we're drivin' right pasture house."*

path·o·log·i·cal (path-ə-lä´-ji-kəl), *n. and adj.* a direction chosen upon reasoned reflection. *"We jus' took the pathological man would take."*

PASTURE

pat·ter (pat´-ər), *v. and n.* to perform a quick, gentle touch, with the flat of the hand, upon a female. *"Sometimes, to let her know I'm available, when my wife walks by I just **patter** on the butt."*

pen·i·cil·lin (pen-ə-sil´-ən), *n. and v.* a writing or drawing instrument that uses ink being offered in exchange for currency. *"I think it's sick that this **penicillin** for two grand!"*

per·so·na (pərs-ōn´-ə), *n. and prep.* a reference to the location of a small strapped satchel usually carried by a woman. *"The cop said if you leave your **persona** table, you're just askin' for trouble."*

pe·so (pā´-sō), *v. and conj.* to provide legal tender in order to move on. *"Will you just **peso** we can leave?"*

pes·ter (pest´-ər), *n. and conj.* an annoying or irritating person, with the rhetorical implication of a non-existent option. *"Is that kid a **pester** what?"*

pet·rol (pet´-rəl), *n. and v.* a domesticated animal performing the rehearsed behavior of turning over. *"Show me a trick. I wanna see your **petrol** over and play dead."*

phar·i·see (far´-ə-sē), *n. and v.* declaring visual cognition of a gathering for trade and entertainment. *"Every time I go to the **pharisee** somebody missin' a finger."*

phar·ma·cy (färm´-ə-sē), *n. and v.* the speaker's visual perception regarding a plot of land used for growing crops or raising livestock. *"Let's hunt behind Jerry's barn, cuz every time I'm at his **pharmacy** deer."*

phrase (frāz´), *prep. and n.* with regard to an increase in salary. *"Will you ask your boss **phrase**?"*

pick·le (pik´-əl), *n. and v.* a prediction concerning a particular choice. *"Slick Rick knows horses real good, so I'm bettin' his **pickle** win."*

PICKLE

PICTURE

pic·ture (pik´-chŭr), *v.* to have pried loose using an appendage or tool. *"Right in front of the whole class you **picture** nose."*

pig·ment (pig´-mənt), *n. and v.* an emotional attribution of past feeling about a particular swine or heavyset person. *"Yeah, I'm cryin'! That **pigment** the world to me. You said we were havin' chicken!"*

pi·lot (pīl´-ət), *v. and n.* to place one thing on top of another. *"My wife was servin' mashed potatoes last night and I said, '**Pilot** on, baby, **pilot** on!' "*

pim·ple (pimp´-əl), *n. and v.* a prediction regarding the future action of a purveyor of prostitution. *"Look, John, you're cute and all, but my **pimple** kill me if I don't charge you full fare."*

pi·o·neer (pī´-ən-ir), *n. and prep.* concerning the location of a crusted pastry. *"This place is called the Pie Hut, man. What do you mean you ain't got no **pioneer**?"*

PIONEER

pi·ous (pī´-əs), *n. and v.* a declarative phrase concerning the state of a baked meat or fruit dish with a crusted pastry top. *"This **pious** so good, God musta made it hisself!"*

pis·tol (pis´-til), *v. and conj.* to continue urination up to a certain moment. *"I drank forty-one beers and I think I could **pistol** the sun comes up."*

piz·za (pēts´-ə), *n. and v.* to make a declarative statement about any person named Peter. *"He loves wearing that dress, man. No doubt about it, that **pizza** weird guy."*

plane (plān´), *v.* being in the act of mischievous frolic. *"I will kill you! Trust me, I ain't **plane** around."*

plan·et (plan´-it), *v. and n.* to organize something in advance. *"Umm, Lieutenant Custer, the next time you decide to take on ten thousand Indians, you might wanna **planet** a little better."*

PLANET

play·wright (plā´-rīt), *v. and adv.* to engage in recreational activity properly. *"I swear I'm gonna bust your heads wide open if you boys don't quit fightin' and playwright."*

pok·er (pok´-ər), *v. and adj.* to jab a female. *"Don't swing that stick at your sister, boy . . . you might poker eye out."*

poo·dle (pü´-dil), *v. and prep.* to defecate up to a particular future time. *"Feed that dog Mexican food and he'll poodle next Tuesday."*

pop·u·late (päp´-yə-lāt), *n. and adv.* the tardiness of a direct male progenitor. *"Populate—I been waitin' for over an hour!"*

po·rous (pȯr´-əs), *v. and n.* to dispense liquid for others. *"Hey, baby doll, could you porous another cup of coffee?"*

port (pȯrt´), *v. and n.* to cause the gravitational transfer of a previously mentioned liquid out of a container. *"Says here, 'Expires 10/02'—should I chuck it or **port**?"*

por·tion (pȯrsh´-ən), *n. and conj.* in addition to an automobile such as a Boxster or Carrera. *"What's the problem, Officer?" "Well, to start, your **portion** you was doin' a hundred and twenty in a school zone."*

post·er (pōs´-tər), *adj. and prep.* acting according to a rule or agreed-upon behavior. *"We ain't **poster** leave until in the mornin'."*

po·ta·to (pət-tā´-tō), *conj. and n.* the inability of a group, regardless of other factors. *"They see us talkin', **potato** know what we're sayin'."*

prais·es (prāz´-əz), *v. and adj.* a male person performing an act of solemn communion with a deity, as connected to something belonging to that male. *"My grandaddy **praises** knees off."*

PORT

PRESSURE

pre·ced·ed (prē-sēd´-əd), *v.* previously sown. *"They ain't ours, Officer. When we bought the house, all those pot plants was **preceded**."*

pres·sure (pre´-shər), *v. and adj.* to apply continual force to something belonging to the one being addressed. *"Just pull out the dart and **pressure** hands down on the wound so we can finish the game."*

pri·ma·ry (prī´-mer-ē), *v. and n.* to exert force on, with the purpose of pulling off or apart, a person with the same name as the mother of Jesus. *"She was so mad, it took four grown men to **primary** off her first husband."*

pri·or (prī´-ər), *v. and n.* to forcibly move a female, using leverage. *"His first wife was so fat, you couldn't **prior** out of the front seat with a crowbar."*

prop·er (präp´-ər), *v. and n.* to lean a woman against an object for the purpose of counteracting gravitational pull. *"A real gentleman wouldn't just **proper** in the corner when she's had too much to drink."*

PROTOCOL

pro·to·col (prō´-tə-kȯl), *n. and v.* a person, paid for his or her expertise, initiating communication. *"Maybe I'll get a **protocol** you and set up some lessons."*

pump·kin (pəmp´-kin), *n. and v.* a declaration about the capabilities of a device used for suctional or compressive transfer of liquid or air. *"No way that little **pumpkin** fill up these tires."*

punc·ture (pənk´-chŭr), *n. and adv.* a declaration concerning an obnoxious youth. *"That **puncture** had a smart mouth."*

quar·ter (kȯrt´-ər), *n. and adj.* a legal tribunal and its effect on or relation to a female person. *"Not only was she drunk, but when she got to **quarter** lawyer was drunk too."*

QUARTER

quar·ter·back (kwȯr´-tər-bak), *n. and adv.* the return of coined currency worth twenty-five cents. *"I'll stop kickin' this thing when I get my **quarterback**."*

quea·sy (kwē´-zē), *v. and adv.* to request restrained enthusiasm. *"**Queasy** on them oysters, boy, you're makin' me sick."*

ques·tion·naire (kwes´-chən-er), *n. and adj.* a particular solicitation of information. *"Where'd I park my car? Now that's a real good **questionnaire**."*

quo·ta (kwōt´-ə), *v.* to relate, word for word, the statement of another. *"To **quota** great philosopher, it's spilt milk under the bridge."*

Rr

rain·bows (rān´-bōz), *v. and adj.* watery precipitation and its relation to a thing or event connected to a person named Beauregard. *"I sure hope it don't **rainbows** weddin' out."*

RATTLE

ran·som (ran´-səm), *v. and adj.* to have conducted certain operations or activities, such as a prescribed series of medical procedures for the purpose of discovering a problem or abnormality. *"I ransom tests and you're fine."*

rap·ture (rap´-chŭr), *n. and adv.* a declarative statement about a form of music combining spoken poetry and repetitive percussion. *"That rapture is playin' loud in that car."*

rat·tle (rat´-il), *n. and v.* predicted behavior from a large rodent of the family Muridae. *"We need to clear the food off this table, or a rattle get at it."*

ra·zor (rāz´-ər), *n. and conj.* an alternative to an increase in salary or wages. *"I told my boss, 'Either you give me a razor I quit!'"*

re·bate (rē´-bāt), *v.* to replace food intended to lure prey, as in a trap or on a hook. *"That fish took your worm, so you're gonna have to rebate."*

RECTIFY

re·cede (rē´-sēd), *v.* to visually perceive a person or thing repeatedly. *"I seed him last Tuesday and then on Thursday I recede him."*

reck·on (rek´-ən), *v.* the ongoing act of destroying or demolishing. *"I keep buying 'em, she keeps reckon 'em."*

rec·ti·fy (rekt-əf-ī), *adj. and conj.* to suppose inebriation after continuing consumption. *"No thanks, barkeep. I'll be completely rectify have another drink."*

re·tard·ed (ri-tärd´-əd), *v. and prep.* to have withdrawn from employment at a particular moment in time. *"This here's the gold watch I got when I retarded age sixty-five."*

righ·teous (rī´-chəs), *n. and adv.* a turn in the dextral direction. *"To get to Route 60 you go up this road about a mile, then make a righteous past the church."*

RIGHTEOUS

rig·id (rij´-əd), *n. and v.* a narrow hilltop and conjecture or suggested possibilities concerning it. *"That
rigid be hard to climb without a pair of stiff-soled boots."*

rig·or·ous (rig´-ər-əs), *n. and conj.* a choice between
a vehicle and a group that includes the speaker. *"I know
you hate to abandon the boat, but it's your rigorous!"*

rit·u·al (rich´-ü-əl), *adj. and v.* a phrase predicting
the actions of a person in the presence of great financial means. *"I know if you ever get ritual buy a yacht the
first day."*

Ro·lex (rōl´-leks), *v. and n.* to move a person who
goes by a nickname for Alex by either turning him
over and over or in a hand-propelled wheeled vehicle.
*"Every night after the bar closes, we gotta Rolex home in
a wheelbarrow."*

ROLEX

Ro·man (rōm´-ən), *v.* to be in the midst of wandering. *"That crazy lady been **Roman** around the coliseum for hours."*

rose·wood (rōz´-wŭd), *n. and v.* agreed-upon activity by a woman named after a flower. *"Tina wouldn't, but **rosewood**, so I married Rose."*

rub·ber (rəb´-ər), *v. and n.* to move one's hand firmly, in a repeated pattern, upon a female. *"To give a massage, **rubber** shoulders like this."*

rug·ged (rəg´-əd), *n. and v.* a woven floor mat or a toupee and conjecture or suggested possibilities for it. *"That **rugged** look better if you cleaned it once in a while."*

ru·mor (rüm´-ər), *n. and conj.* a phrase used in an ultimatum concerning personal space. *"Give me some **rumor** get outta my bed."*

SAHARA

run·ner (rən´-ər), *v. and n.* to repel a female. *"I tried treatin' my girlfriend bad, but I can't seem to* **runner** *off."*

Rus·sian (rəsh´-ən), *v.* acting in a hurried manner. *"Stop* **Russian** *around like a chicken with his head cut off."*

rus·tle (rəs´-əl), *n. and v.* predicted actions of a person named Russell. *"Leave your wallet out like that and I guarantee old* **rustle** *steal it."*

Ss

sad·ist (sayd´-ist), *adj.* the highest degree of sorrow or unhappiness. *"It makes me sad when somebody hurts me, but it makes me* **sadist** *when I hurt somebody else."*

Sa·ha·ra (sə-her´-ə), *v. and n.* a phrase concerning the state or condition of filaments growing from one's epidermis. *"The shave was fine, but it'* **Sahara** *got a problem with."*

saint (sānt´), *n. and v.* to deny or argue against the state of something. *"You just keep on driving along, dude, but I'm tellin' you, saint the right way!"*

salm·on (sam´-ən), *n. and conj.* connecting a person named Samuel to other persons or things. *"Salmon his fishin' buddies have got to leave right now!"*

Sa·mo·an (sə-mō´-ən), *conj. and v.* involving a conclusion about the cutting or thrashing of plants with a bladed machine. *"I like workin' outside, Samoan my lawn ain't no big deal."*

sanc·tum (sank´-təm), *v. and n.* to have caused the submergence of more than one watercraft. *"He took two boats out fishin'. Sanctum both."*

sand·wich (sand´-wich), *n. and pron.* granular soil, usually composed of eroded siliceous rock and commonly found near water, considered in relation to a person or thing. *"My bathing suit was full of sandwich made my butt itch."*

SANDWICH

Sa·rah (ser´-ə), *v. and adv.* interrogative concerning the location or existence of a thing. *"Hey, baby, **Sarah** another beer in the fridge?"*

sat·is·fied (sad´-əs-fīd), *adj. and n.* concerning one's feelings of sorrow. *"When Ralph split with Sadie, I was as **satisfied** divorced her myself."*

sat·u·rate (sat´-chər-rāt), *v. and n.* interrogative about whether or not payment for services rendered is standard. *"**Saturate**, or are you gonna charge me double once you get the job?"*

Sat·ur·day (sat´-ər-dā), *adj. and n.* expressing sorrow about a particular twenty-four-hour period in a female's life. *"Her fiancé didn't show up. It's really **Saturday** got ruined like that."*

sa·vory (sāv´-ər-ē), *v. and conj.* concerning alternatives for a male person and his setting aside of currency for later use. *"He better learn to **savory** will be broke when he's old."*

SCHOOL

scep·ter (sep´-tər), *prep. and adj.* other than something of a female's. *"She came out of the house wearing nothing scepter bra and panties."*

schol·ar (skälh´-ər), *v. and n.* a phrase in which the speaker suggests, to one or more others, telephonic communication with a female. *"Scholar after we've had a few more drinks."*

school (skül´), *v. and adj.* indicating one's sanguinity with a certain situation. *"Sure, man, if you wanna dance with my date, school."*

scoot·er (süt´-ər), *v. and adj.* to slide oneself in any direction while remaining seated, as done by a female. *"Tell your sister to scooter fat butt over so somebody else can sit down."*

scrab·ble (skrab´-əl), *n. and v.* a specific crustacean of the order Decapoda and possibilities for it. *"Scrabble taste real good . . . all we have to do is kill it."*

SCRABBLE

SEAWEED

scur·vy (skər´-vē), *v. and adj.* being the opposite of straight. *"Check out Pam Anderson! Man, that body* **scurvy***."*

sea·food (sē´-füd), *v. and n.* to perceive, through the ocular organs, nutritious substances. *"My problem is whenever I* **seafood***, I eat food."*

sea·weed (sē´-wēd), *v. and n.* to encourage comprehension of the circumstances experienced by the speaker and others. *"We didn't mean to break into your place, but . . .* **seaweed** *been outside in the cold for a long time, and we was freezing."*

se·date (sid-āt´), *v. and n.* to have stated a time four hours before noon or midnight. *"You told me to come at nine o'clock, but Terry* **sedate***."*

sed·i·ment (sed´-ə-mənt), *v.* having stated something about one's intentions or opinions. *"I know what I said, and I know what I meant, but that is not what I* **sediment***."*

se·di·tion (si-di´-shən), *adj. and n.* a specific calculation of the sum of two or more numbers. *"I don't mean to complain, ma'am, but* **sedition** *is real hard!"*

se·di·tious (sed-di´-shəs), *v. and n.* to have verbalized the common name for flat-bottomed or concave containers used to serve food. *"He asked if I wanted to make dinner or do the dishes, and I* **seditious**.*"*

sei·zure (sē´-zhər), *v. and adj.* to match another's bet when gaming or gambling. *"I believe you're bluffin', so I* **seizure** *nickel and raise you ten grand."*

se·nior (sēn-yȯr´), *v. and adj.* to have visually perceived something belonging to another. *"Half the town* **senior** *wife with the gardener."*

se·ño·ra (sān-yȯr´-ə), *v. and n.* regarding current pronouncements about the person being addressed. *"Everybody used to say you was an idiot, but now they* **señora** *dang fool."*

SEDITION

SEPARATE

sen·ti·men·tal (sent-ə-menʹ-təl), *v. and adj.* to have caused telepathic delivery. *"I could pick which card you're thinkin' of, if you **sentimental** picture to me."*

sep·a·rate (sepʹ-ər-āt), *prep. and v.* with the exclusion of a female's consumption. *"Me and her was supposed to share our Happy Meals, **separate** all the fries."*

se·rum (sirʹ-əm), *v. and n.* to char the exterior of more than one thing. *"If you want the steaks to stay juicy, you gotta **serum**."*

sew·er (süʹ-ər), *v. and n.* to take legal action against a female, usually with the purpose of financial redress. *"If she don't give me my money, I'm gonna **sewer** for everything she's got!"*

shad·ed (shādʹ-əd), *n. and v.* used to state that something greatly displeased or was despised by a female. *"My wife tried sushi and **shaded** it."*

SHADED

sheep·herd·er (shē´-pər-dər), *n. and v.* having placed and released an object, as done by a female. *"I can't find 'em now, but I know **sheepherder** shoes right over here."*

shel·lac (shəl-lak´), *n. and v.* a female's future affection for. *"Tell you what, **shellac** you a lot better if you take a bath."*

sher·iff (sher´-əf), *v. and conj.* to offer a portion of, under certain conditions. *"All right, you don't have to **sheriff** you don't wanna."*

Sher·wood (shər´-wŭd), *adv. and v.* an intensive phrase suggesting the certainty of an imagined action. *"It **Sherwood** help if I could get a job with the Forest Service."*

shud·der (shəd´-ər), *v.* indicating regret for a thing or action not done. *"I **shudder** ducked when that guy yelled, 'Duck!' "*

SINCERE

shunt (shənt´), *v. and adv.* indicating that a thing or action was the incorrect one. *"My husband's home—I told you you shunt have come over!"*

side·burns (sīd´-bərnz), *n. and v.* a surface that is afire. *"Leave it on the grill until that sideburns."*

sin·cere (sins´-ir), *v. and adv.* to blaspheme in a particular place. *"If he sincere in church, he's in deep trouble."*

Sin·ga·pore (sing´-ə-pȯr), *v. and n.* to express oneself in song with exuberance. *"When I Singapore my heart into it."*

si·nus (sīn´-əs), *v. and n.* to make a mark of identity needed as proof of approval, for a group. *"Money for medical experiments? Heck yeah, sinus up!"*

SIOUX FALLS

Sioux Falls (sü´-fŏlz), *n. and v.* a person named Susan going from a high position to a lower one because of gravitational pull. *"Sue drinks, **Sioux Falls**."*

si·ren (sī´-rən), *conj. and v.* giving a reason for propelling oneself forward speedily, with a bounding stride. *"That crazy dude came at me with a hammer, **siren** as fast as I could . . . but I guess not fast enough."*

sit·u·ate (si´-chəw-āt), *conj. and v.* a phrase used to explain the consequences of someone else having consumed orally what belonged to the explainer. *"You don't get another piece of pie **situate** mine."*

skil·let (skil´-ət), *n.* acumen for a particular activity. *"I think it's safe to say, son, that you don't have the **skillet** takes to fry eggs."*

sluice (slüs´), *v. and adj.* to declare that a person or thing has escaped. *"My pet python **sluice**!"*

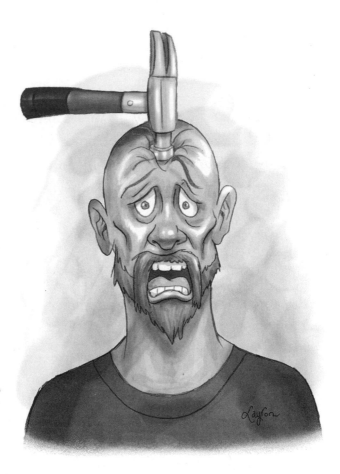

SIREN

snot (snät´), *n. and v.* negating the state of being of a thing. *"Officer, I'm really sorry. I could have sworn that was the guy who cut me off in traffic, but maybe **snot**."*

snow·man (snō´-man), *v. and adv.* to answer in the negative, emphatically. *"If you're askin' did I do it, the answer **snowman**."*

so·cial (sō´-shəl), *conj. and v.* an explanation regarding actions taken to achieve a desired result from a specific female. *"I just gave that doggie some food **social** stop yappin' at me."*

so·da (sō´-də), *adv. and v.* an action or way of being including others. *"I like beer and **soda** my friends."*

Sod·om and Go·mor·rah (sä´-dəm-ənd-gə-mȯr´-ə), *v., n., conj., v., and n.* a phrase describing the ocular perception of more than one thing, plus the resulting action of acquiring additional amounts of those things. *"I didn't have enough doughnuts for my orgy, so when I went to the bakery I **Sodom and Gomorrah** the honey-glazed."*

so·lar (sōl´-ər), *v. and adj.* to effect a change of ownership, in exchange for currency, of a thing possessed by a female. *"I hear old lady Johnson finally solar house."*

sold (sōld´), *adv. and adj.* emphasizing the length of existence. *"If I were a little drunker and she weren't sold, I'd most definitely take a crack at her."*

sol·dier (sōl´-jŭr), *v. and adj.* to have exchanged a person or object belonging to another for money. *"I hope you don't mind, dude, but I soldier mother on eBay."*

sol·emn (säl´-əm), *n. and pron.* a phrase declaring the limit or tally of a number of things or people. *"I expected a bigger turnout at Ken's funeral, but solemn."*

so·lo (sō´-lō), *adv. and adj.* dishonest or morally repugnant, to a certain extent. *"How could you stoop solo as to date my mother?"*

SOLD

SPAIN

soph·ist·ry (säf´-əs-trē); *adj. and n.* an arborescent plant having the smoothest and most pleasing quality to the touch. *"This is the sophistry I ever felt."*

spa (spä´), *v. and n.* interrogative regarding one's direct male progenitor. *"I know Ma's around, but spa here?"*

Spain (spān´), *adj. and n.* a specific sharp physical or emotional discomfort. *"I'm going to the doctor. Spain in my leg won't go away."*

spear (spir´), *n. and v.* stating the presence of an alcoholic beverage made by using yeast to ferment malt and hops. *"We ain't got no wine here, honey. Spear or nothin'."*

spec·ta·tors (spek´-tā-tərz), *v. and n.* to presuppose an encounter with potatoes. *"What will they serve with the roast? I spectators and beans."*

speed (spēd´), *n. and v.* the past tense of a male performing the function of urination. *"He's so drunk, he don't even know **speed** his pants."*

spir·it (spir´-ət), *v. and n.* to stab a creature or an inanimate object with a sharpened staff. *"I ran out of shells, so I hadda **spirit**."*

starch (stärch´), *v. and adj.* to order a person or persons to turn on their motor or motors. *"Gentlemen, **starch** engines."*

star·struck (stär´-strək), *adj., n., and v.* a male person's circular rubber wheel covering coming into violent contact with something. *"He got the blowout when **starstruck** that speed bump."*

stew·ard (stə´-wərd), *v. and n.* a phrase pertaining to specific information or news. *"Hey, what'**steward** on the street?"*

STARSTRUCK

STRIDE

sti·let·to (stə´-let-ō), *adv. and v.* to continue to allow an action of something or someone elderly. *"Sure she's sixty-two, but I **stiletto** lady Thompson climb in my bed once in a while."*

sto·ries (stȯr´-ēz), *n., pron., and v.* a phrase connecting a retail establishment to a male. *"Every time he comes into this **stories** drunk."*

stride (strīd´), *n. and v.* having made attempts in the past. *"He says he can quit smokin' anytime, but **stride** and failed a hundred times."*

strive (strīv´), *n. and v.* a phrase suggesting that one and others operate a motor vehicle; usually used during inebriation. *"Well, we done finished off the keg, so **strive** to Alaska!"*

study (stəd´-ē), *n. and pron.* a virile or sexually active specimen or type in relation to another male. *"He's not half the **study** thinks he is."*

STUPID

stu·pid (stüp´-əd), *n. and v.* to get into a lower position because of the state of a thing. *"I told him, 'Kyle, you better **stupid** is really low.' "*

sui·cide (sü´-ə-sīd), *n. and v.* to agree with the opinion of or position taken by a person named Susan. *"I've heard his side of the story, but it's **suicide** with."*

sum·ma·rize (sə´-mɔr-īz), *n. and v.* to intend or guarantee the fulfillment of an action to be pursued during the months following the June solstice and before the autumnal equinox. *"I almost drowned last August, so this **summarize** gonna learn to swim."*

sum·mer (səm´-ər), *n. and v.* the existence or condition of a subset or part of a group. *"Don't take it personal, Mrs. Herman. **Summer** cute and **summer** just plain ugly."*

SUMMER

sum·mit (səm´-ət), *v. and n.* to review a number of thoughts or themes and synthesize them into a single, unifying concept. *"Well, to **summit** all up, Stan's an idiot."*

sump·tu·ous (səm´-shəs), *n. and adv.* a subset of a group, simply. *"Most folks think he's cool, but **sumptuous** think he's a jerk."*

sun·set (sən´-set), *n. and v.* a male offspring having made a statement. *"I never saw it, but my **sunset** it was the biggest fish he'd ever laid his eyes on."*

su·per (süp´-ər), *n. and conj.* used to indicate a choice between a liquid food made with cooked meats and/or vegetables and another thing. *"**Super** salad?"*

Su·per Bowl (süp´-pər-bōl), *n., prep., and n.* a simmered food in liquid stock in relation to each shallow, concave container in which it is served. *"It's only supposed to be one servin' of **Super Bowl**."*

sur·re·al (sər-rē´-əl), *n. and adv.* used to formally express enthusiasm to a superior. *"Yessir, Sergeant, I'm doin' good, surreal good."*

sur·round (sə-raúnd´), *v. and adv.* used to declare that something is or has been in the general vicinity. *"We done picked up the scent, so I know it surround here someplace."*

su·shi (sü´-shē), *n. and pron.* concerning the actions or response of a female in regard to one named Susan. *"We were gonna get married, but after I told her about sushi changed her mind."*

su·ture (sü´-chər), *v. and n.* to invite another to do as he or she pleases. *"He said he didn't want no anesthetic, and I said suture self."*

sweat·er (swet´-ər), *v. and adj.* to be intimidated by something of a female's. *"Don't sweater rude comments. Just go ahead and ask her out."*

SUTURE

SYCAMORE

syc·a·more (sik´-ə-mȯr), *v. and adv.* to direct an attack with something grander than the original. *"To scare those bad guys you're gonna need to sycamore frightening dog on 'em."*

syn·di·cate (sin´-də-kit), *v., prep., and n.* indicating the location of a thing as enclosed within a container. *"He asked me where my shaving things are, and I told him they'syndicate."*

syn·drome (sin´-drōm), *v. and n.* to dispatch a female to her place of residence. *"If we're at a bar and the wife gets drunk, I just syndrome."*

syn·the·size (sin´-thə-sīz), *n. and v.* a condition pertaining to a thing's mass or quantity. *"It ain't the size of the dog in the fight, synthesize of the fight in the dog."*

tab·leau (tab-lō´), *n. and adj.* a phrase pertaining to controlling the extent of a bill of sale. *"I ain't buyin' another round, 'cause I'm tryin' to keep my **tableau**."*

ta·boo (tə-bü´), *v.* to verbally express negative opinions about another or others. *"It ain't right for them folks **taboo** little Billy like that."*

tal·on (ta´-lən), *v.* to be revealing information verbally. *"I'm **talon** you, it was an eagle, not a hawk."*

tap·es·try (tap´-əs-trē), *v. and n.* to create a canal or opening for the purpose of drainage in a particular woody arborescent perennial. *"You might find some syrup if you **tapestry**."*

tar·na·tion (tär´-nā-shən), *adj. and n.* the complete and total population of a sovereign territorial state. *"The whole country is into NASCAR now. I'm talkin' 'bout the **tarnation**."*

TABOO

TATTOO

tat·too (ta-tü´), *prep. and n.* up to a couple of hours past midday or midnight. *"I can only stay **tattoo**—then I gotta get back to work."*

Tau·rus (tȯr´-əs), *v. and adj.* to rend or split something belonging to a male. *"When he tried to pick up that penny, he **Taurus** underwear."*

taw·dry (tȯ´-drē), *prep. and n.* conveying toward or giving something to any person or creature with the name Audrey. *"If you think the dress is that ugly, why don't you give it **tawdry**? She's half blind, so she'll never know the difference."*

teat (tēt´), *v.* to consume and swallow a solid substance through the mouth. *"Mama, I didn't get enough **teat**."*

tee·pee (tē´-pē), *n.* urination caused by drinking the brewed leaves of *Camellia sinensis*. *"I love drinkin' tea, but after about half a cup I gotta take a **teepee**."*

TELECAST

tele·cast (tel-i-kast´), *conj. and n.* regarding advice given to wait on any action so that it is not done before the deployment of a plaster mold used to ensure the immobility of a limb. *"Don't move your arm **telecast** gets put on it."*

tele·mar·ket·ing (tel´-ə-mär-kə-ting), *v. and adj.* to make a statement to someone or something involved in advertising. *"I once had to **telemarketing** guy that if he called my house one more time I'd hunt him down and shoot his phone."*

tele·path (tel´-ə-path), *conj. and n.* up to a certain time, with regard to a route. *"I ain't hiking no more **telepath** is chosen."*

tele·phone (tel´-ə-fōn), *v. and n.* to recognize or perceive a fact concerning a device that converts acoustic vibrations to a transmittable electronic signal. *"You can **telephone** never rang, 'cuz there's no incoming calls displayed."*

TELEMARKETING

Tel·es·tra·tor (tel´-əs-strāt-ər), *v. and n.* with an implied threat, to command a person to verbalize without prevarication. *"Enough of the bull, boy. Tell us the story and **Telestrator** else."*

tele·vise (tel´-əv-īz), *v. and conj.* to determine one's current state. *"I'm so drunk I can't even **televise** happy or sad."*

ten·der·ize (ten´-dər-īz), *adj. and n.* ocular organs that exude qualities of sympathy and gentleness. *"Her face was mean, but she had **tenderize**."*

ten·e·ment (ten´-ə-mənt), *n. and v.* to intend an integer over nine and under eleven. *"Did I say five? It was **tenement**."*

Ten·nes·see (ten´-ə-sē), *n. and v.* wherein the speaker expresses that he or she visually perceives a thing or person that would earn the highest rating in a decimal system. *"Ben said everyone here's from Nashville, but you're the only **Tennessee**."*

ten·sion (ten´-shən), *n.* mental focus. *"My wife's mad at me 'cause I don't pay her no **tension**."*

ten·u·ous (ten´-yü-əs), *n. and v.* a person's state of being during a past period of life when their age in years, counting from moment of birth, fell between nine and eleven. *"When you was **tenuous** eighty pounds—how in the world did you double that in a year and a half?!"*

ter·race (te´-rəs), *v. and pron.* to pull apart something belong to a male. *"As soon as she saw him she tried to **terrace** clothes off."*

ter·rain (tə-rān´), *prep. and n.* indicating a change bringing the descent of water droplets from a mass of condensed vapor. *"Those clouds could turn **terrain** any second, and this road'll turn to mud."*

ter·ri·fy (tər´-əf-ī), *v. and conj.* to rip apart as a result of certain actions one might take. *"My skirt's so tight, I'm scared it'll **terrify** bend over."*

TENSION

TESTAMENT

ter·ror (ter´-ər), *v. and adj.* to rend or shred something from a woman, usually objects of adornment. *"I couldn't wait to get my wife back to the honeymoon suite so I could **terror** clothes off."*

tes·ta·ment (test´-ə-mənt), *n. and v.* a specific examination, indicated by the speaker's intention. *"When I told you I hope you pass the test, Darlene, that weren't the **testament**."*

tes·ti·fy (test´-əf-ī), *n. and conj.* a written examination, in relation to certain actions one might take. *"I would have studied harder for that **testify** had known it was for half our grade."*

ther·a·py (ther´-ə-pē), *adv. and n.* a phrase connecting urination to a particular time or place. *"Is **therapy** break anytime soon?"*

this·tle (this´-əl), *n. and v.* a prediction about a specific thing or event. *"**Thistle** be easy!"*

tick·le (tik´-əl), *n. and v.* a prediction about the actions of a bloodsucking arachnid. *"If you don't use tweezers, that **tickle** be hard to get out."*

tie-dyed (tī´-dīd), *n. and v.* the expiration of a person named Tyler. *"Ty liked to sleep on the train tracks. Then **tie-dyed**."*

Tif·fa·ny (tif´-ən-ē), *n. and conj.* a fight, with an ensuing reaction by a male. *"My dad and me had a **Tiffany** done cut me out of his will."*

tight (tī´-ət), *v.* to unite or fasten a string, cord, or rope, usually in a knot or bow. *"If you don't want your shoe to come off, you can't go and leave the lace undone like that, son. You've got to **tight**. And when you **tight**, you got to **tight** real tight."*

tile (tī´-əl), *n. and v.* to predict the results of adorning oneself with a fashion accessory worn about the neck. *"Heck, Bubba, this here **tile** get you into any fancy restaurant you want."*

TIE-DYED

TIRE

time (tīm´), *v. and n.* to fasten things together with a knot. *"Don't know what the hell's wrong with my shoes, but I can't seem to time."*

tippy (tip´-ē), *n.* extra money or gratuity paid in exchange for good service, as performed by a male. *"You don't give that waiter a tippy goes crazy."*

tire (tī´-ər), *v. and n.* to restrain a female, as with ribbon, rope, or bungee cord. *"I thought I told you to tire down!"*

tis·sue (tish´-ü), *adv. and n.* a phrase wherein the speaker declares the singularity of the person being spoken to. *"Tissue and me tonight, baby."*

ti·tan (tīt´-ən), *v.* to make more secure. *"Them giant pants wouldn't fall down if you'd titan your belt up."*

TORTURE

tor·toise (tȯrt´-əs), *v. and n.* to have imparted knowledge or wisdom to a group. *"That stupid teacher never **tortoise** nothin'."*

tor·ture (tȯr´-chər), *n. and v.* phrase concerning a person's flame used for lighting a dark area. *"I think there's something wrong with that **torture** holding."*

touch·stone (təch´-stōn), *v. and prep.* to have broached. *"You've done **touchstone** a sensitive subject."*

trac·tor (trakt´-ər), *v. and n.* having traced, hunted, and found a female. *"She ran, but the police **tractor** down."*

tram·po·line (tramp´-pəl-lēn), *n. and v.* a prediction that a destitute person or sexually promiscuous woman will rest against a thing or person. *"First that **trampoline** on ya—then she'll steal your wallet."*

TOUCHSTONE

tra·peze (trap´-ēz), *n. and v.* a device for snaring or capturing prey, connected to a male. *"If he misses the first trapeze gonna fall in the second one for sure."*

trem·or (trem´-ər), *v. and adj.* to cut or shorten something belonging to a female. *"I got all shook up when Cassie asked me to tremor back hair."*

trip (trip´), *v.* to forcibly tear apart. *"First time I saw my wife I wanted trip her dress off and get busy."*

tri·ple (trip´-əl), *n. and v.* a journey and its predicted result. *"If you think Three Mile Island is a nice vacation spot, one triple change your mind."*

tsu·na·mi (su̇-nä´-mē), *conj. and adv.* indicating the reason for an action one is about to take. *"My dang TV just broke, tsunami gotta go get a new one."*

TUNA

tuck·er (tək´-ər), *v. and adj.* to neaten, by pulling something in or by placing one piece of clothing inside another, something of a female's. *"Tell her to **tucker** butt back into her shorts."*

tu·na (tün´-ə), *v. and adj.* to adjust for proper functioning. *"That boy don't say much, but he sure can **tuna** TV right."*

tun·nel (tən´-əl), *n. and v.* a prediction concerning something that weighs two thousand pounds. *"When the waiter asked my wife how much chocolate sauce she wanted on her ice cream, I said a **tunnel** do."*

tur·bine (tər´-bīn), *n. and v.* regarding reaction to a monetary exchange by a female. *"Just 'cause she's a pretty lady, I got no objection **turbine** the next round."*

turn (tərn´), *v.* to obtain deservedly. *"You need to get the basketball through the hoop **turn** points."*

TUNNEL

tu·tor (tü´-tər), *n. and prep.* the consequence or effect of a pair of things. *"One drink just gets her flirty . . . it takes **tutor** get the clothes off."*

twine (twīn), *n.* an alcoholic beverage made from fermented grapes. *"'Twas **twine** talkin'."*

Uu

ud·der (ə´-dər), *adj.* referring to any person or thing that is not the one specified. *"My kid won't drink any milk **udder** than chocolate."*

un·canny (ən-kan´-ē), *prep. and v.* interrogative connecting the abilities of a male to a position over or on top of a particular location. *"It's really weird, but he can't get **uncanny**?"*

uni·sex (yü´-nə-seks), *n. and adj.* a phrase used to connect another with any device or item employed for sensual pleasure. *"Just me,* **unisex** *toy is my idea of a party."*

uni·son (yü´-nə-sən), *n. and conj.* the person being addressed, plus their male offspring. *"Everyone said you was shootin' blanks, man—I never expected to see* **unison.***"*

unit (yü´-nit), *n. and v.* a phrase connecting the one being addressed to the act of creating a garment or other piece of fabric by using yarn and needles. *"Gramma, will* **unit** *me a sweater?"*

unit·ed (yù-nī´-təd), *n. and v.* a British subject being asked about his status regarding a nonhereditary title for excellent public service and merit. *"Hey,* **united** *yet?"*

URINAL

up·raise (əp-rāz´), *prep. and adj.* a vulgar insult to a person named Raymond referring to placing a thing where the sun doesn't shine. *"Up yours, Pete . . . and while I'm at it, upraise, too!"*

uri·nal (yər´-ən-əl), *n. and v.* a declaration concerning the current status or location of the person being spoken to. *"If you think urinal lot of trouble now, just wait till Daddy gets home."*

urine (yər´-ən), *n. and v.* a statement declaring the predicament of another. *"I hate to say it, but if you need to go potty, bud, urine big trouble."*

urol·o·gist (yür-äl´-ə-jist), *n. and v.* a phrase claiming that a group is merely some lesser thing; usually used for the purpose of insult. *"Urologist a bunch of sissies!"*

uti·lize (yü´-təl-īz), *n. and conj.* a connecting phrase concerning the speaker, a temporal condition, and the person being spoken to. *"I was scared to talk to utilize all grown up."*

UTILIZE

va·cant (vā´-kənt), *n. and v.* a group's inability to do something. *"If **vacant** pay, **vacant** stay."*

val·id (val´-əd), *n. and v.* the predicted action of a person named Valentine, Valentino, Valdemar, Valdez, or Valenzuela. *"**Valid** go out with a monkey if you put a dress on it."*

val·i·date (val´-əd-dāt), *n. and v.* the predicted courtship or social engagement of a person named Valentine, Valentino, Valdemar, Valdez, or Valenzuela. *"He's so desperate since that monkey dumped him, now **validate** anything that moves!"*

Val·ium (va´-lē-əm), *n. and v.* a low area between hills, in relation to the speaker. *"I'm too tired to go any farther, so this is the last **Valium** walking through."*

VALID

VESTED INTEREST

van·i·ty (van´-ət-ē), *n. and pron.* indicating past possession by a male of a cargo-carrying vehicle. *"His new van is way nicer than that other **vanity** had."*

ven·ture cap·i·tal (ven´-chər-ka´-pə-til), *adj. and n.* the principal or central place for exciting, extraordinary, and unexpected things. *"I'm tellin' you, man, Las Vegas is the **venture capital** of the whole world!"*

Ve·nus (vē´-nəs), *conj. and n.* indicating action conditional on that of a male plus other persons or things connected to him. *"I'll only go **Venus** friends go."*

ver·ti·go (vər´-ti-gō), *prep. and v.* a conditional negotiation concerning the further movement of a specified female. *"**Vertigo** to the dance I wanna know that she'll be home by midnight."*

vest·ed in·ter·est (vest´-əd-in´-trəst), *n. and v.* a short, sleeveless upper-body garment and the possible curiosity or attention it inspires. *"That **vested interest** me more if Pamela Anderson was wearing it."*

vet·er·an (vet´-ə-rən), *n. and v.* concerning a re-tired soldier or a doctor who administers medical care to animals and the fast pace of his movement. *"That's the same **veteran** over my foot with his Rascal!"*

vir·gin (vər´-jən), *v.* to be approaching or coming close to. *"She's so loose, she's **virgin** on bein' a tramp."*

vi·sor (vīz´-ər), *conj., n., and v.* the start of a speaker's opinion about a particular female. *"**Visor**, I'd lose the baseball cap."*

vi·ta·min (vīt´-əm-ən), *v. and n.* to formally re-quest the presence of a male in an enclosed structure or at a gathering. *"He's your friend, so if you want him at the party, you **vitamin**."*

vix·en (vik´-sən), *v.* preparing. *"We're **vixen** to eat dinner."*

VETERAN

WAITER

wa·fer (wā´-fər), *v. and prep.* to request another person to cease their forward motion. *"Hey, **wafer** me."*

waf·fle (wäf´-əl), *n. and v.* future actions by or state of a female spouse. *"If you want breakfast, my **waffle** make it for you."*

wag·on (wag´-ɔn), *v.* whipping back and forth. *"That dog just bit me in the face, then sat there **wagon** his tail."*

wait·er (wāt´-ər), *v. and conj.* a phrase linking staying in one's current location or delaying action to an alternative. *"I think we'd better **waiter** we're going to be sorry."*

walk·er (wȯk´-ər), *v. and n.* to move on foot alongside a female. *"You be nice to Mamaw and **walker** to the bus stop."*

wal·la·by (wäl´-lə-bē), *n. and v.* the predicted state of the vertical part of a structure. *"That water's already up to your waist, boy. Ain't no way that **wallaby** tall enough to stop it."*

wal·let (wäl´-ət), *conj. and n.* indicating temporal or contradictory conditions. *"**Wallet** appears that I stole your wallet, I didn't."*

ware·hous·es (wer´-haùs-ez), *adv. and n.* a phrase connecting a place to structures for habitation. *"Since the tornado hit, there's just dirt **warehouses** used to be."*

wary (wer´-ē), *adv. and n.* a phrase connecting a place to a male. *"I might be able to get my money back if I knew **wary** lived."*

wa·ter (wät´-ər), *n. and v.* used to introduce an inquiry concerning the future. *"I just wanna know, **water** my options?"*

WATER

wa·ter·front (wät-ər-frənt´), *pron. and n.* used to inquire about the unseen forward-looking side of a female. *"From the back she looks great, but before I ask her out I wanna know **waterfront** looks like."*

wed·ding (we´-din), *v.* making saturated with liquid. *"They been married for seventy years, and now he goes and celebrates by **wedding** his pants."*

Wednes·day (wenz´-dā), *adv. and n.* introducing an inquiry about the future date of an event. *"**Wednesday** we're supposed to get married? 'Cause I might be busy."*

Weed Eat·er (wēd´-ē´-tər), *n. and v.* a phrase indicating past group mastication. *"Every time we were at your grannie's, **Weed Eater** cookies when she wasn't looking."*

whit·en·er (wī´-tin-ər), *adv. and v.* interrogative regarding the past actions of someone or something of a female's. *"If she was sick, **whitener** mother call the school and let them know?"*

WHITEY

whit·ey (wī´-tē), *adv. and n.* introducing an inquiry about the intention of a male's action. *"Aww, **whitey** have to go and do that for?"*

wid·ow (wid´-ō), *n. and v.* a phrase promising future obligation for more than one person, including the speaker. *"I tell you, if you did us this favor, **widow** you big-time."*

Wif·fle (wif´-əl), *n. and v.* regarding the effects of experiencing an unpleasant odor. *"Ole Johnny stinks. One **Wiffle** knock you out."*

wig·gle (wig´-əl), *n. and v.* the future prospects for a prosthetic hairpiece. *"Think this **wiggle** fool 'em?"*

wil·low (wil-ō´), *v. and adj.* introducing an inquiry about the future or future actions of an elderly person. *"I wonder **willow** George Bush do somethin' about the economy?"*

WIGGLE

WINNER

Win·ches·ter (win´-ches-tər), *adv. and n.* at the
time of events involving a person named Chester.
*"We'll eat **Winchester** gets here."*

win·dows (win´-dōz), *adv.* indicating the future
action of a group. *"Hey, Carl, tell me **windows** dogs
come back."*

win·eries (wīn´-ər-ēz), *n. and conj.* a phrase linking an alcoholic beverage made from fermented grapes
to alternative actions of a male person. *"Just get him
another glass of **wineries** gonna start making a scene."*

win·ner (win´-ər), *adv. and adj.* with temporal regard to someone or something connected to a female.
*"Tell me **winner** car pulls into the driveway."*

win·ter (wint´-ər), *v. and adj.* regarding the past
movements of a female. *"She **winter** way and I went
mine."*

wire (wī´-ər), *adv. and n.* introducing an inquiry as to the motivation of or reason for an action. *"So, uh, **wire** you here?"*

wis·dom (wiz´-dəm), *v. and n.* to urinate more than one thing. *"My uncle had two kidney stones, but he **wisdom** both out."*

won·der (wən´-dər), *n. and prep.* indicating action concerning a specific person. *"If you need a good taxidermist, he's the **wonder** call."*

wood·en (wü´-dən), *v.* to have fervent desire for an event not to occur. *"I can tell you I **wooden** want her as my wife."*

wor·ri·some (wər´-ē-səm), *v. and n.* a subjunctive phrase regarding a male's state or condition. *"I'd have been anxious **worrisome** sort of jerk."*

WISDOM

WORRY

wor·ry (wər´-ē), *adv. and n.* regarding the location of a male. *"No, I don't got no idea **worry** went."*

wres·tle (res´-əl), *n. and v.* indicating or predicting the future effects of a period of inactivity. *"A full night's **wrestle** do you good."*

wrin·kle (rink´-əl), *n. and v.* a prediction involving an icy surface used for skating. *"I'm gonna throw my little girl an ice-skating party, and this **wrinkle** work great!"*

Xe·rox (zē´-räks), *v. and n.* to visually perceive solid mineral material. *"I ain't divin', 'cause I **Xerox**!"*

X-ray (eks´-rā), *n.* the former spouse of a person named Raymond. *"That's one of Ray's exes, but she ain't the **X-ray** was talkin' about."*

xy·lene (zī´-lēn), *n. and v.* to incline one's body. *"He hurt me with his left hook, 'cuz **xylene** to the right."*

yacht (yät´), *n. and v.* to advise or urge someone toward making a wise choice. *"**Yacht** to put out that cigarette while you're pumpin' gas."*

ya·hoo (yä-hü´), *interj. and pron.* interrogative regarding which person or persons. *"Shut up?! **Yahoo** is gonna come over here and make me?!"*

Yaht·zee (yät´-zē), *n. and v.* suggesting that a person visually perceive something. *"Oh man, **Yahtzee** the booty on Tiny's wife!"*

Yale (yāl´), *v.* to emit vocal tones at a high volume. *"I heard you the first time. You don't have to **Yale**."*

YAHTZEE

yar·mul·ke (yä´-mə-kə), *pron. and v.* a reference to something a person or group has created. *"No doubt about it, Rabbi Steinberg, **yarmulke** mean margarita."*

yawn (yȯn´), *n. and prep.* indicating the position of another. *"Watch where you're steppin'! **Yawn** my foot!"*

yearn (yərn´), *n. and v.* interrogative concerning the financial compensation a person obtained in exchange for labor. *"**Yearn** anything last year?"*

yel·low (ye´-lō), *interj.* a greeting. *"**Yellow**!"*

Yid·dish (yi-dish´), *n.* a vessel designed for the holding and carrying of food; specifically, such an object of a particular person. *"Where are your manners?! Take **Yiddish** to the kitchen when you're finished!"*

ZANY

yon·der (yänd´-ər), *v. and n.* an involuntary intake of air and widening of the mouth, performed by a female. *"At her start of her interview she had the job, but then she **yonder** way out of it."*

You·Tube (yü´-tüb), *adj. and n.* a stretchy cylindrical article of clothing belonging to the person being addressed. *"Put on **YouTube** top, baby, we're goin' out someplace nice tonight!"*

Yu·ca·tán (yü-kə-tan´), *n. and v.* allowing for the ability of another person to expose their epidermis to the sun's rays for a period of time, causing it to darken in hue. *"It's your choice: **Yucatán** in a booth or **Yucatán** at the beach."*

za·ny (zā´-nē), *v. and n.* indicating another's proclamations. *"This guy was standin' right here the whole time, and now he's **zany** didn't see nothin'."*

ZION

ze·roed (zē´-rōd), *n. and v.* a male who has just traveled, as on the back of an animal. *"Screw him and the horse **zeroed** on."*

Zi·on (zī´-ən), *n. and prep.* regarding the orientation of a male's ocular organ. *"He's had his **Zion** Betty-Lynn all night."*

zit (zit´), *v. and n.* interrogative regarding the effect of a specific thing. *"Mama, this pimple on my forehead—**zit** gonna ruin my date?"*

ZIT

About the Author

JEFF FOXWORTHY is the largest-selling comedy-recording artist in history, a multiple Grammy Award nominee, and the bestselling author of more than twenty books. He is the host of the hit Fox television show *Are You Smarter Than a 5th Grader?* His syndicated weekly radio show, *The Foxworthy Countdown,* is carried in more than 220 markets across the United States. He lives with his wife and two daughters in Atlanta.

About the Type

This book was set in Berling. Designed in 1951 by Karl Erik Forsberg for the Typefoundry Berlingska Stilgjuteri AB in Lund, Sweden, it was released the same year in foundry type by H. Berthold AG. A classic old-face design, its generous proportions and inclined serifs make it highly legible.